Look Back,
But
Don't Stare

a memoir

Look Back, But Don't Stare

a memoir

Mary Lou Edwards

A
GREAT FIRE
PRESS
PUBLICATION

PUBLISHED WORKS

Little Did We Know: Making the Write Impression
You Couldn't Make This Up

HavingtheLastWordStories.com
MLEDWARDS.COM

Library of Congress Cataloging in Publication Data

Edwards, Mary Lou
    Look Back, But Don't Stare
p. cm.
Published by Great Fire Press
ISBN: 978-0615603407
Library of Congress Control Number: 2012938543

Some of the names and identifying characteristics have been changed to
protect the privacy of the individuals involved.

Cover design by Caroline M. Edwards.

To my Mother who danced backward to music she did not write, lived stories she never told and made sure I would be able to do both.

Grazie . . .

Table of Contents

Normal is just a setting on a
washing machine.

— Anonymous

. . . when it first walks into his grave little head
that adults do not always have divine intelligence,
that their judgements are not always wise,
their thinking true, their sentences just – his world
falls into panic desolation. The gods are fallen . . .

— John Steinbeck

Table of Contents

*The best hope is that one of these days
the ground will get disgusted enough
just to walk away leaving people with nothing
more to stand on than what they have so
bloody well stood for up to now.*

— Patchen

*Don't compromise yourself.
You are all you've got.*

— Janis Joplin

Look Back, But Don't Stare

Don't Stare

a memoir

Normal is just a setting on a washing machine.

— *Anonymous*

The Harmonica Battle

Music lessons were always a bone of contention in our house. According to the Gospel of My Father, who was never, ever wrong my cousins had taken music lessons, but alas, after forcing their parents to pay a fortune to a music teacher, invest in an albatross of an instrument and waste time at recitals, they no longer played.

The litany of the musical ingrates reverberated at dinner whenever the subject of music lessons was on the table. Rosie took lessons for years; she no longer touches the keyboard. Concetta had a promising musical career which she willy-nilly threw out the window. Josie absolutely refused to practice and even pleading could not coax Angie to play a single note, irrefutable proof that music lessons were a waste.

If the saga of the ingrate cousins did not quell our creative urge, my father shared his tragic trumpet experience. He'd swapped his life's treasures to pay for the hospital deliveries of his children. His first born forced him to abandon his motorcycle; when I came along he had to surrender his sailboat, and his beloved trumpet was relinquished with the arrival of our baby sister.

I thought my father got taken. There was no equating my brother with a Harley, and I'd not have sold even part ownership of a sailboat for me. As for my sister, suffice it to say that she was not worth a broken guitar string, never mind a trumpet. So because of his few bad deals, we were never going to make the sounds of music.

No, siree, Bob, in our house there'd be no guitars nor trumpets, no music lessons period. End of discussion. End of subject.

Until the fifth grade when love knocked on my door.

I developed a major crush on a boy whose ex-Marine father gave weekly harmonica lessons in our church basement. For five dollars, I could purchase a Marine Band Hohner Harmonica, and for an additional dollar a week, I could share a group lesson, and sit next to my dream boat. With Mormon-like zeal, I embarked on a relentless campaign to convince my father that harmonica lessons were essential for human development methodically obliterating his every objection. After a couple of weeks of my determined and heartrending offensive, the embargo was lifted. The fact that the instrument would be plastered to my mouth rendering me speechless, at least during practice was, more than likely, the biggest selling point.

For more than a month, I was faithful to my music. I was seated next to my heartthrob and so in love that I found even his droplets of spittle, which came flying my way, romantic. Copious amounts of spittle are the natural by-product of good harmonica technique, and my Romeo was always whacking his instrument clearing his blow holes. Not thinking that particularly feminine, I didn't whack my harmonica, and I suspect that slowed my musical progress. Still I was no ordinary girl hammering out "Chopsticks" on the keyboard, nor a run of the mill accordion player squeezing out "Lady of Spain." I was mastering our Forefathers' Hit Parade – "Red River Valley," "She'll be Coming Round the Mountain" and "Oh, Susanna."

Then, just as the accolades were in sight, just as I was mastering "Old Black Joe," my adored idol dropped the class. I was devastated. Not only did my vision of international fame evaporate but my musical passion vanished with Mr. Cool not even knowing my name. My goal of becoming the Paganini of the mouth organ was over, dead.

"Dad," I said as I subtly approached the subject of ending my musical career, "you were absolutely right. Music lessons are not all they're cracked up to be. They're highly overrated, and the dollar a week is eating up my allowance."

"Don't even think about quitting!" he growled, heading me off at the pass. "You are just now mastering 'I've Been Working on the Railroad,' and 'She'll Be Coming Round the Mountain' needs only a little more polishing."

My father was obviously delusional. This was not going to be easy.

"Besides," he added, "Your instrument is paid for – you're not wasting all that money."

"You have got to be kidding," I gasped, knowing he wasn't. "It's only a pocket Marine Band Harmonica for crying out loud! It only cost five dollars, Dad! It's not like it's a giant baby grand piano plunked down in the middle of our living room," I ranted. "Besides I'm not really that good. In fact, I'm actually terrible. Mr. Capidimonte said that my 'Turkey in the Straw' is the worst he's ever heard."

"Is that so? Well, that's because you don't practice enough. From now on you're going to practice for an hour a day! Mary,'" he yelled to my mother, "see to it that she practices everyday for an hour before I get home from work!"

I could not believe this was happening. I had really shot myself in the foot on this caper, and now I was to suffer a fate worse than a shot in the heart. Not only was I suffering the trauma of a romance gone bad, but my father, with his perverse sense of retribution, was going to make his little Yankee Doodle Dandy pay for her artistic subterfuge. His insensitivity appalled me.

Did he not realize that I'd gotten into this jam because I was a fifth-grader in love? Would he not allow his own flesh and blood who'd been blinded by a gigolo to extricate herself from a collapsed dream? Could he not sense that I'd been jilted and had to get on with my life?

Dropping the harmonica now became my raison d'être. Persuading my father to let me abandon my bogus career became an obsessive mission. It was obvious that this Herculean task required more than my usual techniques of relentless badgering, pathetic pleading and persistent whining. It was painfully clear I was involved in a battle of the wills.

Neither age, nor gender, nor family rank was on my side. I needed a really creative strategy.

The answer to my prayers came after a novena to St. Francis Borgia, Patron Saint of Deception and Duplicity. It dawned on me that my father wanted me to practice for an hour every day after school because he did not want to hear the off-key din, he did not want to listen to the noise, the racket. The light bulb went on; I could torture him with my playing! I could use my harmonica as a weapon!

Every day after school I'd busy myself with Girl Scouts, cleaning the church altars, helping the nuns, fulfilling my Patrol Girl duties – whatever it took to delay music practice until after supper. I would head to my room just as dad pushed away from the table to digest his meal, and I'd start blowing into the old harmonica.

And every night I'd play the same song for one solid hour straight.

One night it would be a screechy, "When the Saints Come Marching In." The next night it would be a mournful, out-of-tune hour of "Old Black Joe."

Once, after about forty-five minutes of "Swing Low Sweet Chariot," my mother came barging into my bedroom actually threatening me. "Keep it up," she warned, "and I'll make you swallow that damn kazoo!"

She had never been supportive of my musical ambitions even when I had stardust in my eyes, now she was downright hostile. "I know what you're trying to do, you little scheming brat!" she hissed. "You'd better stop that racket right now and start blowing some different tunes!"

Narrowing my eyes and raising my eyebrows, I'd snip, "It is not a kazoo. It is called either a harmonica or a mouth organ." And I'd rev up the cacophony.

"Jim, I can't take this anymore!" she would shriek to my father as she tied a dishtowel tightly around her head, a medical procedure she learned from one of her wacko cousins, to contain the pain of a splitting headache. "This is a nightmare! You must make her stop! I beg you!"

My father, never one to be sympathetic to his wife's complaints, nor anyone else's for that matter, had yet to see through my battle plan.

4

"Mary, she works on a single song because she must perfect it. Music requires practice and dedication."

"Dedication my foot. You've been predicting since she was four that she'd be a lawyer because she's so devious. Can't you see she doesn't want lessons – that she intends to drive us crazy so that we'll beg her to quit?"

I had to hand it to my mother. She was one smart cannoli.

Before long though my father did begin to catch on to my unusual form of waterboarding. He started to crack and then, one day, he finally went off the deep end.

"Mary Louise, I am warning you. You'd better stop with that "Swanee River" screeching immediately or you'll be sorry," he muttered with twitching jaw muscles. "Switch right now to a different song, you little witch."

So I switched, to "Danny Boy." Italians loathe "Danny Boy."

That did the trick.

Within minutes, my harmonica was a worthless piece of twisted metal.

Disgusting Four-Letter Words

My friend, Domenica, maintained that after a woman got married, if she kept a clean house and didn't get fat, she could be an axe murderer and no one would care. Men reserved a particular scorn for wives who did not keep a house spic and span or who, God forbid, "let themselves go," but I feared the scorn of men far less than I feared household drudgery which I suspected caused brain damage. Polish furniture that was already shining? Scrub floors that weren't even scuffed? Launder clean curtains just because it was Monday? *I don't think so.*

I considered housework a form of domestic violence and C-O-O-K, I-R-O-N, and D-U-S-T offensive four-letter words. My aversion was not genetic. My mother's housekeeping made Polish cleaning women look like slackers and she was a world-class cook on top of it. 'Til today I

7

rarely eat in an Italian restaurant since no dish ever comes even kind of close to hers.

I could claim I was intimidated by her extraordinary culinary skills, but I'd be lying. The truth was preparing, cooking, and cleaning up three times a day for a family that considered memorable meals an inalienable birthright, was just not part of my plan. I was not going to be trapped in a kitchen.

It wasn't as though my mother didn't try to steer me toward domesticity.

"Mary Lou," she'd say as she stirred at the stove, "come watch how I do this."

"I'll know how you did it when I eat it, Ma," I'd respond, trying to dodge the bullet.

"No, you need to see how I make it. Someday you'll be sorry you didn't learn how to do this."

"Ma, I told you I'm going to college. I don't need to know how to cook."

"Don't be stupid, college people eat. What are you going to do when you get married?"

"I probably won't get married and, if I do, I'll find a man who's not that into food. Or I'll marry someone who likes to eat out," I said, thinking of solutions on the spot. "Then again, maybe we'll just eat at your house every night or my husband will cook like daddy."

"Cook like your father?" she responded, her eyebrows leaping to the ceiling.

"I saw daddy make eggs for breakfast once."

"It was probably when Nonna was dying and I was sitting vigil at the hospital."

"Well, it was the only time I ever saw him cook, but you never know. Look at Bo."

My father's friend, Bo, made the best sopresatta in the world. To this day, not here or in Italy, have I ever found anything that could compare to his air-dried mini-salamis hanging by their strings in his attic.

"I could marry a chef. Ma, did you know women can't be chefs?" I said, trying to take the spotlight off my recalcitrance. "I read that all of the world's great chefs are men."

"Sure," my mother agreed, "when it's a man cooking they call him a chef and pay him big money. Mothers, who make great food every day, are just plain old cooks."

"But, Mom," I teased, pecking her on the cheek, "you get paid in love."

"I know. I know. I'm a lucky woman," she smiled. "I always wanted to be a wife and mother. I'm not complaining."

You should complain I thought. *If I were you, I'd be complaining big-time.* What is so rewarding about having 'floors you could eat off of' or shining kitchen tile with Jubilee every week?

Perhaps none of this appealed to me because I was a disaster at it. Even when I tried, I got it all wrong.

Once I attempted to help my mother with the ironing, but I had no sooner dug into the bushel basket when she yanked the iron cord from its socket.

"Your father would never wear such wrinkly underwear plus you scorched a pillowcase. You're impossible," she railed, as she collapsed the ironing board with a thud almost amputating my fingers. If I'd known that a burned pillowcase would be my ticket to freedom, I'd have scorched from the get-go.

Momma was right though – I was impossibly incompetent. I couldn't even hang laundry right. I let the sheets drag on the grass because I forgot to use the pole to prop up the clothesline. I hung the socks by the ankle instead of the toes. I mixed articles of clothing instead of grouping them. And my towel hanging was a complete disgrace.

"Look at how you hang towels," she said with disgust. "You're using two clothespins for every towel and wasting clothesline between them."

"Ma, you make it sound like there's a clothespin shortage." And I wanted to add, *you have enough clothesline for the entire family to hang themselves*, but I knew when I was walking on thin ice so I kept my mouth shut.

9

"Keep it up, Mary Lou, and you're going to be in real trouble. Try following directions, for a change. Put one towel on the line and put a clothespin in the left corner," she demonstrated, "then instead of wasting another clothespin, take the second towel and lap it over the first a tiny bit and use another clothespin to hold the two together, then add another towel and do the same thing and keep going until you've hung all the towels together. For every two towels you should only use three clothespins. I'll watch you finish this row."

"Ma, you have got to be kidding? This is moronic," I argued, "I can't believe you expect me to do this. Let's just throw on a few extra clothespins and really live it up."

"Capo tosto! You're such a hardhead, you never listen," she scolded. "You think everything's a joke. You're hanging things willy-nilly. Put all the handkerchiefs together, all the dishtowels together." Lowering her voice to a stage whisper, she added, "And hang the underpants on the inside clothesline where the whole world can't see them."

"Mother," I protested, "I think the neighbors *know* we wear underpants and brassieres. I mean, *what's the big secret*?"

"Shame on you – panties are private, hide them on the inside. Put the sheets and towels on the outside lines so the sun can get at them, and quit being a smart-aleck."

I hated the tasks I was given, and I was always deemed too young for the jobs I coveted.

I yearned to sit on the windowsill, my legs dangling in the house, my torso outside, and pull the window sash down on my lap to squeegee. Jenny Next Door used to sit almost totally outside on her third floor sill holding onto the frame with one hand, squirting her vinegar spray bottle with the other while her long black hair blew in the breeze. Gawking from my backporch, letting my Popsicle drip on my pedalpushers, I was amazed at her courage, mesmerized by her dexterity. Once, and I am not kidding, *she even stood up outside on the window sill to reach the upper sash*, one hand holding on, the other swiping the rag back and forth over the glass, all the while yelling at her sons down in the yard who were chasing each other with a hammer. It was like watching a tightrope walker cross the Grand Canyon.

"Ma," I begged, "please, if you let me wash windows sitting half outside like Jenny Next Door, I promise I'll make them sparkle."

"No," she said, "you have to be at least fourteen to do that. The last thing I need is to find your body crumpled in the gangway. People would never stop talking and you'd probably leave the windows streaky."

"We live on the first floor, for crying out loud," I whined. "I'll pull the window down tight on my thighs. You just don't want me to have any fun."

"Knowing you, Sarah Bernhardt, you'll fall out the window and crack your skull just to get attention, and I'll get stuck sitting with you in the hospital. You can run around on window ledges all you want after you're married and your husband has to worry about you."

I think she knew, before I knew, that my ineptitude was a subversive form of passive resistance. Somewhere deep inside my little noggin I must have realized that if I excelled at domesticity, I'd be signing my own death warrant. My mother, however, attributed my aversion to a " . . . combination of laziness and reading too many damn books." She refused to accept that I was beyond domestication.

One of her last ditch efforts was registering me for eight weeks of sewing lessons at the Salvation Army Settlement House, commonly known as "The Sal" where mostly non-Catholic urchins ran amok, but my mother was desperate. Perhaps she thought she'd appeal to my creative side but, alas, I continually jammed the sewing machine while trying to fashion her Mother's Day gift of a tea apron. I assured the teacher my mom did not need a tea apron because she only drank coffee, but Mrs. Muscolino snarled, "You are making a tea apron and your mother will love it!" In the eleventh hour, when I burned out the pedal on the sewing machine, Mrs. M took pity and gave me a needle and thread, but I had no luck with that either so I opted to staple on the waist ties. I considered glue, but I figured staples would hold up better knowing my mother's propensity for obsessive laundering.

My teacher checked over the finished product. "What exactly do you think your mother is going to be putting in this pocket? It's huge – almost as big as the apron. And the waist ties? They're supposed to be *equal* in length." Whipping off her measuring tape from around her neck, she said, "One of the ties is four inches, the-other-is-fourteen. Unless your mother has the waist of a wasp, this will *never* fit her."

"Well, if the ties are too short she can give it to the lady upstairs. Her baby could use it as a bib," I suggested, vowing never to sew another blessed thing as long as I lived.

On Mother's Day, after we gobbled up the delicious frittata my mother cooked for the special occasion, my brother, sister and I brought out our presents.

She opened my brother's first.

He gave her a breathtaking Our Lady of Fatima statue. Our Lady was standing on a blue plastic ball which my brother said was the world. I could see how he thought that, because it was round like the Earth, but it was all blue and everyone knew the Earth was only two-thirds water.

"I don't think it's the Earth, there's no *land*," I snapped, jealous that my mother was acting like he gave her a relic from the Vatican. Shooting me a dirty look and completely ignoring my input, my brother played his trump card.

"Ma, twist the globe – it opens." Sure enough, she twisted and this huge black rosary fell out of the Earth. "Anthony," she exclaimed, "I will treasure this forever." He stood there beaming like an altar boy who gets to lead the casket out of the church after a funeral. I felt like snapping Our Lady off her perch, but I was not going to commit a Mortal Sin and risk going to Hell because of my brother. It was always obvious my mother adored him just because he was her first-born and only son. As far as she was concerned he could do no wrong, and she rarely punished him for anything. Once I saw him actually walk into our kitchen with his muddy baseball spikes on, and she barely yelled at him. The truth was if he had given her an elbow macaroni necklace, she'd have been just as over the moon so I pretended I didn't care, but secretly I had to admit it was a very cool present. The way the Earth twisted open around the equator, and the giant rosary beads fell out, was extremely impressive.

My sister gave mom a floral handkerchief on which she'd embroidered MOTHER. I didn't think it was a big deal but my mother said, "Oh, Anna, this is just what I needed. How did you know?" as though she didn't have an entire drawer full of cleaned and pressed hankies.

"Open mine, open mine, Ma, I sewed it just for you at the Sal," I said, thinking perhaps I should have evened out the waist ties before I wrapped it. My mother opened the box and pulled out the apron from the tissue paper. "Ohhhhh, isn't this an *interesting* apron," she said, as though I'd given her a stupid pencil holder made out of a tuna fish can.

My brother, still smarting from the fact that I had pointed out Our Lady of Fatima was not standing on the Earth, interjected, "Apron? It looks like a cockeyed shopping bag, if you ask me. She didn't even sew it – it's a bunch of staples."

"No one asked you, Anthony," my mother said, shooting him the evil eye. "I'm sure your sister worked very hard on this."

As my father sat at the kitchen table with a "what the hell is that" look on his face (he was into details like measuring and neatness) my mother looked up from the tea apron and said quietly, "Mary Lou, you must stay on the Honor Roll and do well in school. You will never make it as a housewife."

After the apron caper, little was asked of me outside of picking up dog crap in our yard, running errands and drying dishes.

I could see I was a huge disappointment to my mother. She was getting very close to the final stage of grief, acceptance. Now I seriously began to beg for God's help with my domestic disability.

"Dear God, Please send me a rich husband so we can have a housekeeper. My mother has told You over and over *'God, this girl will never learn to do housework!'* and You know she is right. It would be nice if he's handsome, smart and likes to have fun too but, really, the maid thing is the most important. I have to go to college first, but please start looking now because everyone says it's going to be impossible to find a husband interested in a wife who only wants to read books all day. If you can't find a rich one at least find one who doesn't care about home-cooked food. AMEN."

I said that prayer often, and it worked, sort of. God sent me a husband with all my requirements, except he was not rich, but, here is where I knew God was really on the job, my mother-in-law had been such a horrible cook my husband thought Cheerios with a banana was a gourmet dinner. If I so much as made toast, which I didn't do often, he was grateful. Thanks to peanut butter and jelly, lunchmeat, cereal and carry-out, we did just fine. Occasionally I went all out and cooked, but I always seemed to miss the mark.

In a fit of madness one day, I decided to make fried smelts for supper. I have no idea what possessed me, but it sounded easy enough when I overheard someone say you just put oil in a frying pan and throw in the smelts. Had I done this *and* stayed in the kitchen, we might have actually had a home-cooked meal. Instead, someone called in need of a phone number which I went upstairs to retrieve. As I stood on the landing returning to the kitchen, phone number in hand, black smoke billowed up the stairwell. Taking a deep breath, I flew down the stairs and out the front door, sooty and shaking.

Standing across the street from my house, I saw the smoke pouring out the front door, and I just knew my husband was going to be furious. Several months earlier, he had been really aggravated when the microwave door blew off while I was sterilizing my contact lenses, and that little caper had only involved replacing the microwave and patching a hole in the wall. I was sure he'd be over the top if the house burned down. Fortunately a neighbor called the Fire Department and the hook and ladder arrived minutes before my husband pulled up and jumped out of his car leaving it in the middle of the street.

At least a dozen firemen charged through the front door, giant boots flapping, pick-axes at the ready, smashing out windows.

"What happened? Where's my wife?" my husband shouted as I came charging across the street to explain.

"Are you okay? What happened?" he hollered amidst the chaos. "Did something explode? Were you smoking? What's going on?" he asked as the flames waved hello out the kitchen window.

Just then the fire chief, in a huge rubber raincoat with Chicago Fire Department emblazoned on the back, walked toward us.

"Don't worry, sir. We've got this under control," he reassured my husband. "It's a run-of-the-mill kitchen fire – lot of smoke, not too much damage. We knocked out some windows and the cabinets are shot, but it looks worse than it is." Turning to me, he said, "And you, little woman, better be more careful when you're cooking dinner."

"Cooking dinner?" my husband choked out, his eyes the size of pizza pans. "*You were cooking? In the kitchen? At the stove?*"

"Yes," I said. "Yes, I was frying smelts."

"Frying smelts? Like fish smelts?"

"Yes, I wanted to surprise you by frying smelts."

"What in God's name were you thinking? Smelts? We've never had smelts. I cannot believe that you were trying to cook smelts?"

I was getting a bit annoyed with his shock and disbelief, acting like I'd never stepped foot in the kitchen. Was he forgetting I had almost savant-like talents for making chicken wings? Was he blocking on the fact that one Thanksgiving I cooked a turkey which wreaked havoc with everyone's digestive tract? It was not as though I never cooked.

"I wanted to surprise you by frying smelts," I sniveled. "They're not that hard to make."

"Not that hard? You've practically burned down the freakin' house. Whatever possessed you?"

"I don't know," I said shrugging, "all of a sudden I felt like cooking. Is that such a sin?" I wanted to add *you ungrateful bastard* but the neighbors were crowding around, jumping over the fire hoses ostensibly to comfort us, but really to be nosy. "I can't explain what came over me."

A year prior when we were having the kitchen redone, the remodeler was peppering me with questions. "So what kind of fridge do you want? Side by side, freezer at the top, ice-maker on the door? Cold water dispenser? Twenty-four cubic feet?"

"Look," I had told him, "I just want a plain old refrigerator. I'm not really into kitchens. If I had my way, we'd turn this room into a den, but my husband says that would hurt the resale value."

"Yeah," he had said, "most buyers are lookin' for a kitchen."

So we put in the new kitchen, and now it was in shambles.

"Promise me, look into my eyes and promise me you'll never do this again," my husband pleaded as the firemen gave the all-clear sign. "You could have been incinerated."

"Okay, alright, I promise," I assured him. "If the smelts had turned out, I was going to bake you a birthday cake next week but now I won't even bother."

"Good. That's why God invented bakeries."

About six months later, in another fit of impulsive recklessness, I decided to make an egg.

"Honey," I yelled, "have you seen my frying pan? I've searched everywhere."

With a look of alarm, he walked into the kitchen. "Yes, I did see the frying pan. Do you remember when you set the house on fire frying smelts?"

His tone of voice suggested I was some kind of demented pyromaniac.

"Well, during the blaze," he continued in a Mr. Roger's voice, "the firemen threw the skillet out the window. When the snow melted in the Spring, I found the pan and threw it in the garbage. Is this the first time you've noticed it's gone?"

Apparently he'd forgotten he made me promise not to cook so I ignored his snide remark.

"Thanks a lot," I snipped, highly insulted. "You at least could have told me it was trashed. That was a very expensive frying pan I got for my shower and I hardly used it. Now I have to go to the hardware store and buy another one. How am I supposed to make an egg with no pan?"

"You're not supposed to," he said. "Grab your coat. M-E-N-U is not a bad four-letter word."

Blueprint for an Eating Disorder

My brother, our family's first-born, had been finicky, only five pounds, colicky, a fussy eater. A strange baby for our family said my father's three sisters who were in the habit of birthing jumbo jets.

When he was a week old, my father's eldest sister placed her two-month-old daughter, nine pounds at birth and gaining weight at warp speed, on the bed next to her new cousin.

"Oh my God!" my aunt exclaimed, "We've never had such a scrawny, pathetic baby in our family! How did this happen? He doesn't even look like he belongs to us."

Humiliated by the stamp of maternal failure, my mother vowed to rectify her mistake. She devoted herself to straining liver, mashing vegetables and pureeing perfect fruits to fatten him, hoping to make him worthy of the arrogant aunts, the arbiters of family acceptance.

My mom should have spared herself, my brother gained not an ounce. Tony, the neighborhood druggist, prescribed weight gain tonics and appetite enhancers to no avail. The thin, bony infant developed into a slender

17

little boy – adorable and bright, true, but shockingly "skinny and scrawny" lamented the crones.

Four years later my Mother was given an opportunity to atone for her sins. Again pregnant, she made novenas, not for a boy or a girl, but for a healthy baby that would eat. God answered her prayers.

Encouraged by the entire family, I was a "good eater" who redeemed my mother of her previous ignominy. I ate solids before I had teeth – eschewing mushy cereal in favor of pizza – a fabulous achievement. I preferred pasta to a pacifier. By age four, I could eat almost as much as a grown-up, cause for applause. I never refused seconds and always had room for more. I could eat dinner at home, supper at my Big Nonna's, a snack at Little Grandma's, biscotti and milk at bedtime – all in one night.

I was a veritable mini-eating machine. I put my monkey-jawed brother to shame as his cheeks puffed full of macerated food he refused to swallow.

"Okay, chew all night and you won't go to Kiddieland," my mother would threaten during dinner. "Look at your sister – she finished everything on her plate – such a good girl!"

My mother alternately lobbed shots of admonishment and approval, threats and compliments back and forth like some schizoid game of table tennis. "Please, Honey, eat," she pleaded, "Your sister ate her dessert and yours too because you didn't finish your meat."

Her head swiveled between the two of us as the drama of good and evil played out in front of Daddy, the scorekeeper, who cheered every swallow.

For all of the disappointment and aggravation my brother's eternal cud-chewing brought, my gobbling locked in my title as undefeated eating champion – a title that was not in the slightest way threatened even by the arrival of my baby sister. My chubby cheeks, wrinkly thighs and robust health clearly signaled that this sturdy twig would strengthen the hallowed family tree. The drones were forced to reconsider their original disdain for my mother's genetic contribution.

"She is gorgeous," they exclaimed, "A perfect cherub! Look at those pudgy, strong legs! She's beautiful!" they cooed as I waddled about cookie in hand.

Then the cookie crumbled.

We almost never went to the doctor. Other than measles and mumps, we were healthy and, for the occasional sniffles, there was always Tony at Gabric's Drug Store.

Once, however, my sister, seventeen months younger than I, became lethargic and developed a croupy cough that wouldn't go away. Alarmed, my parents decided that a trip to the North Side – a world away – was in order to consult with our real doctor, the one who'd delivered us.

Russell Barrett M.D. was a massive, silver-haired general practitioner in the days before each body part had its own specialist. When not delivering babies, he amputated arms, repaired varicose veins, corrected crooked spines, cut out tonsils, healed ulcers and generally fixed whatever was broken. He diagnosed by sight and sound rather than textbooks and his booming pronouncements were indisputable though his expertise left something to be desired when dealing with the psyche. Once when my mom, whose daily responsibilities included the care of her terminally ill mother, octogenarian grandparents, perfectionist husband and three kids under the age of six, mentioned she was feeling a bit swamped, Doc prescribed she go downtown and buy a hat. That she had not a minute to breathe, was financially pressed, physically drained, mentally exhausted and emotionally depleted apparently escaped his medical radar. But he'd delivered three healthy babies, and had initials after his name so he had a lock on his sacrosanct status.

Dr. Barrett had seen neither my sister nor me since birth. As we entered his office for her appointment, his megaphone voice thundered,

"My God, what took you so long to bring her in – she looks awful!"

My mother was taken aback. "Does she really look that bad?"

"Bad?" he roared, "She's a mess. How could you allow this to get so out of control? This is a shame!

"Well," my Dad countered, "she's only been really pale the last day or two."

19

"Day or two?" he hollered, "This doesn't happen to a kid in a couple of days. Put her on the scale."

And, for the first time, everyone present realized he was talking about me.

"No, no, no, Dr. Barrett, we're here for the little one," my mother protested, "she's almost lost her voice from coughing so much."

"She'll be fine," he decided with a cursory glance at my sister as he rolled his chair back from the scale to his desk. "This one is in serious trouble."

My parents attempted to mount a defense.

"Doc, she's smart as a whip – her vocabulary is astonishing. She reads the Tribune to her Nonna all the time," my Dad offered.

"That's irrelevant – she weighs too much," he responded dismissively while scribbling on his chart.

"But she's a good swimmer and jumps double-dutch better than ten year old girls," my Mother proffered. "She's quite a gymnast – does birds' nests on the rings."

"She's five and she's fat. The rest is unimportant. Put her on a diet!" he roared. "No more cake, no candy, no sweets, period! Do you hear me, Mother? Nothing in between meals, no snacks, no bread, cut out desserts. Are you listening, Mother? No cookies, skim milk, eliminate second helpings. I want to see a different kid in front of me when you bring her back in eight weeks."

He was glaring at my mother and had really worked himself into a lather. I wanted to ask my brother if a doctor has a heart attack does he go to another doctor or can he fix his heart himself, but then I figured my brother would say I was stupid so I just stared at the doctor's jacket which had Russell Barrett, M.D. written in red thread above a little pocket.

"What about the little one?" my Mother thought to ask.

"She'll be fine. Put a vaporizer on at night," Dr. God ordered as our family trooped to the front desk to make a new appointment.

I had a million questions leaving the doctor's office. Why didn't Dr. Barrett pay attention to my sister who was really the sick one? Why didn't the big fatso go on a diet himself if it was such a great thing? Why did he shout at mommy and not say anything to daddy? Why didn't it matter that I was smart and could read and swim? How could I change into a different kid? How do you lose fat – where does it go?

All these concerns were whirling in my head, but my mother looked very sad, and I didn't want to bother her with questions so I just whispered, "I'm sorry the doctor was mean to you. I promise I will stay on my diet so he never yells at you anymore." She squeezed my hand. "Really, Momma, you will never be ashamed of me again. I won't ever get you in trouble." She gave me a little, tiny smile that made me want to cry, but I couldn't cry and make her feel worse.

I had no idea, that over the years, the worst was yet to come for me.

The emaciated look of models and movie stars was speeding into vogue and voluptuous women were admired only in Rubens' paintings. Overweight kids reflected on a mother asleep at the wheel so there was no time to waste in preparing a girl for one-size-fits-most.

With the metamorphosis scheduled in eight weeks, the diet had to be fast-tracked and the scale god would decide my fate forevermore. In a culture that prized chubby babies, but looked askance at plump kindergartners, where mangia, mangia was a mantra, the goal would be a challenge.

Counting calories ranked right up there with counting blessings, and while health was important, image was almost on par so if lecturing, shaming and restricting were what it took to protect little butterballs from cookie jars and candy bars that was the way the ball bounced.

Overnight the fat little girl became the family's designated obsession.

No sooner had we gotten back to our car than my brother began what would become a childhood of sibling taunts.

"You can't go with Daddy to the drugstore for Green Rivers anymore!" he sneered. "You can't have milkshakes at David's or stop the Good Humor Man when he comes down our street," the teasing continued. "You can't have Italian lemonade when we go to Taylor Street because you are a fatty, fatty two by four!"

With this my mother, who adored her first-born son, reached over the back seat and smacked him in the mouth.

21

That slap was no match for the emotional hit I'd suffered.

At age five, I lost twenty pounds. My brother and sister gleefully consumed any contraband that accidentally came my way and snitched about any they were too slow to snatch from my hands. "We're only trying to help you. We don't want you to be a tub of lard," they sing-songed as they policed my every mouthful.

Everyone contributed her two cents about my diet, my body, me. My dad bragged they'd caught "it" in time. Sister Lucille, my kindergarten teacher, said now I could swing on the monkey-bars. Neighbors raved they didn't know me anymore. My Godmother said now my new body matched my beautiful face. Even the milkman said he didn't recognize me.

But not everyone agreed.

"Madonna mia!" the harridans lamented, "she used to be so gorgeous," assuming, I suppose, my hearing had disappeared along with the weight. My friend, Connie, said she liked me just fine the way I used to be. The man at the shoestore asked if I'd been sick. Nonna wondered where her baby had gone. "You're disappearing before my eyes," she said in broken English.

No one noticed in the swirl of conflicting opinions my biggest loss had nothing to do with pounds. All of the qualities that had been praised and valued no longer mattered – being me was not good enough. The blueprint for an eating disorder had been drawn and the foundation built of words, mortared with mixed messages, would last a lifetime.

Worried About the Soft Spot

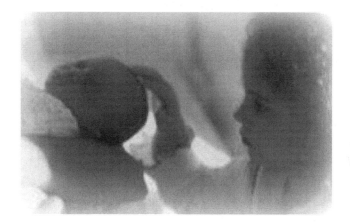

I'd held a baby only once before when I begged my mother to let me hold my brand new cousin. "First wash your hands, then sit on the sofa," she ordered. She put Laura in my arms and knelt in front of us. "Hold your thighs together so you make a lap. Support her neck, prop up her head, keep your arm under her body, don't breathe in her face. Careful when you kiss her, watch out for her soft spot."

"What's a soft spot?" I asked.

"It's the part of her head that covers her brain. Now lower your voice or you'll startle her."

Laura started to wail. "Here, take her back, babies have too many rules."

I steered clear of babies after that and then it happened again.

"Here, my phone is ringing, hold her for a second," my neighbor Lucy said as she thrust her baby, Kiki, into my arms. I was only five years old, a tiny kid myself, sitting on the stoop and munching on a Snicker's.

I pressed my thighs together to make a lap like I remembered from Laura and, poof, just like that, Kiki flipped out of my arms. I gripped her ankle; her pink rubber pants flashed the whole neighborhood. Clutching her leg, I hoisted her up to eye level. Lucky thing her brain didn't fall out of the soft spot. When I flipped her right-side up, she looked okay. Her face was as bright red as a flaming-hot jawbreaker, but her bonnet was still stuck on her head, and she wasn't bleeding.

"Kiki," I scolded, "you can't just do a somersault whenever you feel like it." Kiki was screaming and not paying attention.

"I don't know why she's crying, maybe she missed you," I lied to Lucy, who hadn't seen her baby bungee-jump from my arms. I was glad Kiki couldn't tell her mother that she was twirling around upside down and almost bounced on the sidewalk.

Over the years, worrying about Kiki's brain caused me many sleepless nights. My brother's friend, Stevie, went to the hospital after he jumped off his garage roof while playing Superman. My brother, who was very smart, said Stevie had a concussion which meant his brain got jiggled in his skull. Even though Kiki hadn't hit the ground, I knew her brain had a good jiggle. Would she grow up to be normal?

"Whatever happened to Stevie after his concussion?" I asked.

"He got in trouble for playing on the roof, and his dad punished him."

"I mean what happened to his brain. Did he like start acting weird?"

"You're weird," my brother sneered, as he rode off on his Schwinn. "Something's wrong with your brain."

So all I could do was spy on Kiki to see if her brain was working right. Every time I'd see Lucy with her in the buggy outside, I'd push the mosquito netting aside and peer at her little bald head.

"How is she today, Lucy? Has she started to talk yet?"

"Oh, Sweetie, she won't be talking for a while. She's still too little."

I wanted to tell Lucy that, thanks to me, Kiki might never talk. I worried that she might get stuck in kindergarten for a couple of years because she had trouble learning then she'd end up like Butchie, down the street. My brother said Butchie was slow because he'd been dropped on his head when he was a baby. Butchie had to repeat second grade *twice*.

Being on the alert for signs of brain-damage was complicated by the fact that Kiki's family was strange to begin with – I mean, her brother's name was Jujube. Jujube! All the boys in our neighborhood had names like Joey or Junior – no one was named after candy that you bought when you went to the movies. On top of that, Jujube's ears were lopsided, and he kind of looked like he might not make it past fifth grade. To further complicate matters, Kiki and Jujube had different fathers because my brother said Lucy was divorced which meant she traded in her old husband for a new one. So it was going to be hard to know if Kiki was goofed up because of me or her loony tribe. I worried that I was going to have to take the whole blame if Kiki didn't turn out right, if she couldn't spell or add or subtract.

When I was seven, my Nonna died and we moved into her old flat six blocks away. Though I didn't change schools, I did lose track of Kiki. I always prayed, though, that she turned out to be normal and that someday I could tell her it was an accident and please forgive me. I dreamed of explaining to Kiki that if she had brain problems it was partly her fault for acting like a kangaroo.

Kiki's caper set me up for a life of chronic worry, but, in fairness to her, I did go to Catholic schools where hijacking cerebellums and embedding neurons of fear was an art form.

At the age of seven, my First Confession, the day before my First Holy Communion, kicked off a deluge of anxiety when I toddled into the black hole of a confessional. A weekly Examination of Conscience required searching out every sin committed in thought, word and/or deed, by acts of commission or omission, intentionally or accidentally, either consciously or unconsciously, in rain, sleet or snow, in sickness or health, pre-conception or postmortem.

"Bless me, Father, for I have sinned . . ." was my Saturday afternoon mantra, a ritual that was supposed to " . . . stop God from crying over all the bad things you did during the week," said Sister Perpetua. I thought God must be nuts to cry because I'd rolled my eyeballs at my mother when she told me to dry the dishes. But just after I thought about the possibility of God being cuckoo, I realized the thought was sacrilegious so I'd wait in church all afternoon until the priests changed shifts and the refugee Croation priest, who spoke almost no English, came on duty. No matter what you confessed, he'd say, "Okay, tree r fodder, tree Hey, Marys. Go."

25

That I accomplished anything in school was astounding seeing that I was so busy dissecting, analyzing and seeking second opinions from my girlfriends on the gravity of my sins.

"Josephine, I know snitching is a sin, but what if I snitched on my brother because I heard him use a swear word? I don't think it's a sin because it did stop him from saying Hell." "Well, you just committed a sin yourself because you said the "H" word," said the pint-sized Elmer Gantry. "Plus snitching is a sin no matter what your brother did."

"Another sin just because I said the "H" word?"

"Yes, but it's just a Venial – you only go to "H" for Mortals," she said.

I ran to Confession, and was relieved when I smelled beer through the little screen which meant Father Alky was on the other side. He probably didn't know what rolling eyeballs were since he too had language limitations. But then I worried that if he didn't understand me, his forgiveness wouldn't count so I added yet another sin by lying that I'd left my prayer book in the pew and fled.

I ran across the vestibule, and got in Father Steve's line. He too had escaped the Communists and his English was not the best, however, he was up on the latest sins. Sometimes you'd be waiting your turn and you'd hear him bellow, "YOU DEED WHAT?" Within minutes you'd see a blubbering eight-year-old exit, and run down the aisle with his jacket pulled over his head hoping not to be identified. One time Peter Manzino crashed right into the baptismal font as he tried to make a break for it. Sister Praxeda caught him and dragged him back to the box. Pushing Peter to the front of the line, she made him go in and confess that he'd broken the baptismal watering hole. This time Father Steve's "YOU DEED WHAT?" shook the choir loft. I went in right after Peter, and the kneeler was all wet. I pretended it was holy water.

Over the next few years, my repertoire of sins expanded. Envy, wrath and eavesdropping reared their heads when my brother turned sixteen and got his first part-time job and a paycheck. His tales about the shoplifters, quick-change artists and crazy customers caused me to covet his exciting life.

Then came the day I had long prayed for: a Kiki update. Her mother popped up at my brother's store.

"Ma, remember Lucy, our old neighbor – Jujube's mom? She came shopping today."

My Dumbo ears flapped at the mention of Lucy's name.

"Oh, I haven't seen her in ages. How is she?" my Mom asked.

"She's fine; she has a new husband and another baby."

"How's Kiki?" I blurted. "Is she alive?"

"Well, *yeah*," he said with a *you are such a knucklehead* look. "Most people are still alive in fourth grade."

"I meant to say is she normal?"

"Yeah, I guess so," he said, "but they don't call her Kiki anymore – she's Katherine, and Jujube only answers to Jerome. He's studying to be a detective."

"Good for him," my mother said.

"Yeah, it is, but Lucy's really braggy. She said *detective* like it was a big deal."

"It is a big deal," I chimed in. "She probably thought that with his un-even ears he'd never make it through school. But what did she say about Kiki?"

"Katherine," he corrected me, and turned back to Mom. "Mom, do you ever brag about me?"

"No," she said as she greased a pie pan. "Your father and I don't be-lieve in it. We expect you to do well, and we don't need to advertise."

"I get it, but I'd appreciate a little bragging once in a while."

I agreed. "You could at least say something like my daughter is very intelligent."

"Ma can't say that because she doesn't want to lie," he smirked. And then he dropped a bit of gossip that was intended to make me jealous, but instead took a ton of weight off my heart. "Lucy said Katherine got to be May Crowning Queen because she got straight A's."

"Straight A's?" I screamed, "You're kidding! Kiki, straight A's – May Crowning Queen – wooohoo!" Bubbles of shock, disbelief, gratitude and relief fizzed in my head. "That's the best! I can't believe it! Go, Kiki, go!"

"Mom, she is psycho," he said, his lip curled like Dukey our landlord's mean dog. "I'm positive that one day when you weren't looking, someone dropped her on her head."

The Torture Hour

The nervous snickers started the minute my father opened the cedar-lined closets doors and dragged out the behemoth Magnavox reel-to-reel tape recorder. As my mother rushed to serve a masterpiece guaranteed to jump start every salivary gland on the planet, the pleading began.

"Please, Mom," my brother begged, "not another music appreciation dinner."

"Be careful, this is hot. Don't touch," she'd caution, as wisps of steam rose from the bubbly gravy and stringy mozzarella entree.

"C'mon, Mom, he's right. You hate it too," I'd hiss. "Be honest, make him stop."

"You kids better be quiet," Mom would warn, giving us a take-no-prisoners look. "Not everybody gets to have dinner music."

By then Dad had threaded the magnetic tape on the huge circular wheels, and took his seat at the head of the table. As we bowed our heads for the requisite murmuring, "Bless us, O Lord, for these Thy gifts..." the torture hour began.

With the loud click of the PLAY button, the air was filled with "ana one, ana two, ana three . . ." Once again, Lawrence Welk and his band of acoustic terrorists were ruining our dinner with the "Beer Barrel Polka" and his Champagne Lady of Music was holding us hostage with "I'm Forever Blowing Bubbles."

By the end of the first song, agita had a stomachhold.

With each grating, offensive squeak of the string assassins, my brother would grimace and do his best cowboy rendition of taking a bullet in the heart, I'd trill the lyrics, and my sister would buzz like a kazoo. My mother acted as though everyone was running a normal temperature despite the fact that even our mutt, Skipper skittered off to a prior engagement.

Before *Mairzy doats and dozy doats and liddle lamzy divey* was finished, the dinner hour would have deteriorated into a Monty Python episode. *My father's* steely-eyed glares of disgust along with the scary implications of his *You kids just keep it up* threat served only to ratchet up the idiocy. Despite our desperate attempts to suppress the hysteria, the absurd lyrics, cheesy accordion/organ duets and Welk's inane show-biz patter would inevitably result in my brother's always impressive coup de gras, spewing milk from his nose. My mother's feeble attempts to bring order to the court served only to provoke my father even further, particularly if her efforts interrupted one of his favorites like the *Hoop-Dee-Doo Polka.*

Occasionally my brother got lucky with his milk-spout nose, and my father would send him to his room, but, if my dad was really ticked off, he made him stay at the table and continue to be tortured.

Jabbing the STOP button, dad would launch into a lecture about insolence and ingratitude interspersed with, "You brats, don't know good music." I always thought it peculiar that he considered us the dimwits when it was Welk who said things like "Myron and I will now do a solo together."

Once the maestro announced that he was going to play a song from World War Eye.

"What's World War Eye?" I asked, only having heard of World Wars I and II.

"Don't ruin this song," my father snapped while *If You Were the Only Girl in the World* reverberated throughout the kitchen.

I later read that Welk thought the roman numeral one on his cue card was a capital I.

The English language was just another piece of the collateral damage.

Life Has To Be Hard

Life has to be hard. Not life *was* hard or life *is* hard or life *can be*
hard. No, *life has to be hard.*
This was my father's mantra.

The tragedy of the Great Depression, experienced as a teen-ager,
would become his forever filter for the future, proof that God intended
life to be grueling. Hard work was the protectant, enjoyment the enemy.

He acknowledged God's gifts, but dared not savor them because life
had to be a struggle and the Great Scorekeeper kept a sharp eye out for
those who searched for the easy way. A God who deprived the
undeserving, punished the ungrateful and exacted a price from those who
didn't use their gifts correctly was not to be crossed. And because some
people were not listening, despite Matthew, Mark, Luke and John having
spread The Word, He deputized my father His translator.

In the deaf community, there is a huge debate about the responsibilities of the translator. Does the translator relay the exact message of
the deaf or a sanitized version? Does the translator communicate only the

literal or tinker with intent, and, beyond that, does the translator interject what he thinks the deaf person really meant to say? My father did all of the above and knew we were all pathetic scofflaws, and in the colloquial sense, deaf and dumb too.

He interpreted what God meant – what God intended – what God wanted. In fact, his pipeline was so direct, he understood what God demanded even before God knew, and, because the Deity was preoccupied with wreaking economic havoc around the world and sorting through the wreckage, dad, familiar with the drill, filled the vacuum. Whether a trifling matter or major issue, he never strayed from the message – life has to be hard.

One didn't really know how to drive unless the car was stick shift nor eat a genuine sandwich unless the bread was homemade. A four inch footing was insufficient for a proper concrete patio, a three foot pit had to be dug. A week's vacation involved mending broken screen doors, fixing appliances that were on their last legs and repairing squeaky floor boards in a rented summer cottage. Picnics required homebaked cakes and hauling four-course meals a mile, under scorching sun and over burning sand, down to the beach. The inside of a refinished dresser drawer had to be as flawless as the top. And all because, in order to grow, in order to really live, life had to be hard. The tougher it was, the better one was, the closer one came to earning life's gifts and God's approval.

Swimming, biking, ice skating, chess were not pastimes; they were skills to be perfected through effort and practice. Hobbies were a waste of time unless one intended to incorporate them into a career.

College students, according to dad's Gospel, needed to study two hours a night for each scheduled credit hour. In response to his constant badgering that I was a bogus scholar, who really didn't value, care about, want, and/or appreciate an education, I attempted to reason with him.

"Dad," I tried to explain, "I carry 16 hours a semester. I'd have to study 32 hours a night."

"Do you think they're just going to hand you a diploma? Do you think life is a cakewalk?"

How silly of me to think good grades indicated sufficient study when only blood, sweat and tears could provide real validation. How stupid of me to forget life had to be a bitch.

When life got too good, as sometimes happened, Dad would temper it with shame. Shame was the antidote to toxic enjoyment. Shame was the "go-to" emotion that ensured one never forgot that life had to be hard.

As a kid, my brother was quite a good baseball player. He did not brag about it, but he made the fatal mistake of being comfortable with his competence, confident of his skill and talent. Life was good for a twelve-year-old gifted athlete – maybe too good. He needed to be cut down to size. He had to pay for his adolescent cockiness. He needed to know that life was hard and, if he was not getting the message, then God would teach him and the great translator would deliver the news.

Once during a ballgame, my brother knocked the winning run out of the park. Thrilled with his accomplishment, he sauntered around the bases basking in the admiration of the crowd. My father was incensed and awaited him at home plate. Yanking my brother by the shirt, he shouted, "Who do you think you are? You need to hustle, move your ass around that field – run like you mean it!"

One can only imagine the embarrassment and humiliation my brother felt at being criticized and ridiculed in front of the crowd. But God wasn't finished – sometimes life had to be extra hard.

Grabbing my brother by the uniform, God dragged him over to the coach. "Don't count that run in the score," he ordered. "That homerun doesn't count. The kid didn't earn it, he doesn't appreciate it. Take it off the board!"

Suddenly it was no longer about the winning homerun. It was about God running amok.

The boys on the team crowded around stunned. The spectators watched in amazement. The coach glared in disbelief. My mother stood frozen.

Actually, it was all my brother's fault for forgetting that life had to be hard. God had no choice but to teach him a lesson, had no choice but to etch that reminder on his young psyche.

Dad continued to carry the message everywhere and never missed an opportunity to educate. One really didn't *deserve* to be on the honor roll, a degree earned at a world-class institution was *a fluke* and one scored a great job because the employer had yet *to find you out*.

But as I grew, I started to question my father's "no matter what you do it's never good enough and you must always work harder" ethic. Despite his thinking we kids hadn't worked hard enough for the honor roll, we consistently made it so it couldn't have been by chance. Some slackers probably made it through university, but most degrees were hard won. Could it be that human beings weren't supposed to be perfect?

And then I heard about Louie Aparicio hitting a homerun and swaggering around the bases at a White Sox game. Perhaps life didn't have to be hard. Perhaps life is only as hard as you make it.

Not Every Woman's Dream

Long ago there lived a girl named Thumbelisa who did not want to be a bride. Actually, it was not being a bride that bothered her, it was marriage, but Thumbelisa lived at a time when most maidens became brides, when it was very important to be married.

Thumbelisa had studied the ancient civilizations and was not impressed with the Greeks who believed it ". . . a woman's duty to remain indoors and be obedient to her husband" nor with the Romans who declared "...a woman had no rights. In law she remained forever a child." Then there was the Jewish law that said ". . . a wife was owned by her husband." Even when she dismissed these notions as relics of the past and set aside the biblical teachings that 'a wife was to submit to a husband,' 'he will dominate you,' 'you are subject to him,' she was still looking at wives in the village who were overworked, underappreciated, overwhelmed and undervalued. No, Thumbelisa thought, this is not something I want to do.

Her culture, however, dictated three choices – nun, spinster, wife. Exist under God's thumb, suffer under the King's thumb or languish under the Master's thumb? She couldn't fathom being dictated to by the Pope, perishing in a convent, or subsisting as an old maid forced to live with the King forever, so, by default, it was marriage. But, adding insult to injury, Thumbelisa had not even a poor prospect, let alone a worthwhile catch. "Settling" was out of the question. Bad enough to shoot her future from a cannon without tethering it to someone she'd "settled for" 'til death do us part.

She'd had a bit of a reprieve because the King believed every maiden should be educated – an unusual notion in the old kingdom. His theory was a maiden needed an education *to fall back on in case she married a louse,* not the most sterling of reasons to pursue learning, but she was not one to stand on ceremony. School bought her time. Her family had always said, "Oh, she's the one into books, not boys . . ." as though she had to choose between knowledge and knuckleheads, but schooling did postpone the moment of truth. Now, though, her education was complete, and she was eligible.

Thumbelisa considered running away, but leaving the village was treasonous so she prayed to the patron saint of Good Marriages. And, before she even finished the nine day novena, a prospect appeared whose manner suggested he had no interest in using his thumbs for anything other than a gesture of encouragement, an ally who prized an independent woman. He was an impressive egalitarian – handsome, tall and distinguished – with a great sense of humor.

She began to consider taking that leap of faith.

She was not so naïve to think him perfect. She'd been raised by King Perfect and that was a harrowing journey.

From the outside, they were almost a comic study in opposites – tall/short, blonde/brunette, WASP/ethnic, agnostic/Catholic, reserved/ brash. Yet though they differed in background, politics, personalities and demeanor, their hearts were of the same mold. They shared many a shortcoming, complementary ones too. Neither entertained the notion of changing the other, in part because they were smart enough to know that would be futile, but also because both understood "as is."

"If we wed," she would declare, "I must keep my checking account, have my own coach, work outside the castle..."

That's up to thee, if that is what thou desires, he would respond, wondering how the seed of dread had been planted.

"Also," she would persist, "Can we vow to love, honor and respect, instead of obey?"

"It is called wedlock," he reassured, "but you will not be imprisoned."

For the first time, she trusted the journey could be equally rewarding.

A critical detail remained, the King's imprimatur

"Are you sure you know what you're doing?" the King cross-examined when the Knight asked for Thumbelisa's hand in marriage. "She is an awful lot of trouble, very strong willed – almost impossible to control, challenges orders, resists direction," he ranted. "You will have your hands full. Are you up to the task?"

"Marriage is a privilege, not a task," the Knight responded, understanding more clearly the roots of his maiden's apprehension.

He realized why she wanted the hoopla over quickly – how a long waiting period might provoke anxiety, cause her to doubt her choice, allow her fears to implode.

Fortunately, though the King was vexed at the suddeness of the event, annoyed that he was not in charge and quite displeased that the Knight was not of his choosing, he did appreciate that he would be divesting himself of a thorn in his side and so he consented.

They would wed the following month. The event would have just enough trappings to keep the villagers' tongues from wagging. There would be no engagement ring, a borrowed wedding gown, no bridesmaids, simple gold bands, a banquet small by kingdom standards. They would omit the word *obey*.

The eve preceding the nuptials arrived. King Perfect, issued one final order to Thumbelisa. "Inform the Knight that he is to be rid of his beard for the ceremony. I would prefer a clean-shaven face," he declared.

"He is perfect just the way he is," she replied and the morning after, Thumbelisa and the Knight exchanged hearts.

Wed or Dead

In our house, *a girl*, no matter how old, left her parents' home either wed or dead. Since I was neither, my father created a third category, *running away*, defined as a daughter's act of shameful rebellion, betrayal, ancestral treason.

My father often referenced " . . . the time she ran away." Those unfamiliar with the saga would raise their eyebrows in puzzlement; others, accustomed to his histrionics, would sigh.

After college graduation, I lived at home while I taught and saved to fund a dream trip, a summer in Europe. After my travels, I intended to get an apartment, though I had no idea how I'd make my escape. While going out on my own was as much a part of my *here I come, world* plan as my European tour, I knew the subject would be inflammatory; it took little to ignite conflagration.

With dorm living, a college degree, travel and a good job under my belt, I felt equipped to leave the nest despite my father's opposition.

Mary Lou Edwards

After way too many dinner table wars, the lines were drawn – *it's my life* versus *over my dead body*. The rhetoric was hot, mine trumpeted independence, his loaded with dire predictions. You'll be mixing with strangers, you're putting yourself in harm's way, there are drug addicts out there, you could get mugged and robbed, he prophesied. Men will hit on you, he said. That particular caveat I hoped went from his mouth straight to God's ear, but the other warnings I packed away in the *if you cross your eyes, they will stay that way* category.

My married brother got wind of the escalating hostility, and suggested an unusual strategy.

"Pack your bags and go. He's never going to give you permission, if that's what you're waiting for, so just do it. You're not a hostage."

I could not have been more astonished had he suggested I hook up with a Satanic cult. Perhaps because of his gender, my brother never internalized the fact that females in our house were subject to different rules, some made up on the spot. True, I wasn't physically captive, but just walking out, the notion that I could just do it, was unfathomable. My college girlfriends went out on their own, but that was because, according to my father's script, their families didn't care, didn't value their reputations, were shameless and amoral. After awhile longer under my father's thumb, I became willing to take my chances, and the seduction of independence trumped fear.

I *ran away.*

Impervious to the warnings that I was risking my life, asking for trouble and tempting fate, sharing a flat with Beth, a college acquaintance, whose paramour had walked out of her heart and out on their lease, seemed perfect. I needed to bring nothing more to the furnished apartment than my suitcase, two boxes and three garbage bags of earthly possessions. Soon though, I discovered, that part of Beth's emotional healing involved bringing home strangers she met in bars. Mornings, I was afraid to walk out of my bedroom not knowing if she'd run off to work leaving her man of the hour eating breakfast at our table. Facing a potential Mr. Goodbar was terrifying, particularly after I overheard a colleague say that she'd awakened one morning to find that her one-night stand had absconded with all of her jewelry. Accused by Beth of not understanding how one recovers from a shattered romance, I took to locking my bedroom door at all times, and being alert for strangers in our shower. I slept over at a friend's apartment on nights when the prospect of Beth mending her broken heart seemed likely.

Thrilled when the lease expired, I signed on with Carri, a dorm friend, whom I knew to be neither desperate, needy nor prone to falling in love with strangers after two drinks. The only problematic part of our living together was the fact that we were both very messy, our preferred description – not dirty messy, not disgusting messy, just sloppy spirits who thought housekeeping a waste of time, slackers who used chairs as closets, and figured college diplomas immunized against household drudgery. Reading won hands-down when the alternative was vacuuming, and we didn't own anything worth polishing so we, like Thing One and Thing Two, were comfortable in our little pigpen littered with newspapers, running shoes and lesson plans.

One day I returned from teaching unable to unlock the front door. After ten minutes of fiddling with the key, I called our building janitor, who showed up an hour later with his nine-year-old clone, disgruntled that I'd interrupted his happy hour.

I tell you, Helmet, womens stupid, always trouble, I heard him grumbling to his son as they climbed the stairs to find me sitting on the floor outside my apartment.

"Mr. Hormet, my key's not working," I said. "The door won't open."

He jerked my key ring from my hands, and proceeded to lecture me on the art of unlocking a door. He had no luck either.

"Door bar," he barked.

"Can't be, I was the last one out this morning, and I locked the door."

"Door bar, maybe burglar home," he guffawed. "Helmet, go back door!"

Within minutes, Helmet appeared in the doorway crowing, "The back door was wide open! Your house is wrecked!"

"See," Mr. Hormet triumphed, "I tol' you robbed!"

"Oh, God," I shrieked, "What happened? What the hell happened?"

43

"You been robbed," Helmet screeched, delighted to be a player in the drama. "I discovered the crime. I'm like a detective – you have to tip me!" His father concurred, "Yeah, big tip!" The notion flashed through my mind that Mr. Hormet might be the culprit, but just as quickly I realized that he could never stay on task long enough to cause such destruction.

The apartment was a catastrophe – drawers dumped, closet contents strewn about, furniture upended, pictures ripped off walls, potted plants smashed – ruined, destroyed, trashed. Couldn't someone tell from our thrift-store decor that this was not a Gold Coast apartment, that we had nothing of value?

"How could this be," I lamented to the officer who responded to the 911 call. "Nothing here is worth stealing."

"Even a camera or a radio is a jackpot for a drug addict, Miss. It's $20. – more than he had before he picked your lock."

As I sat in tears, the detectives arrived to dust for fingerprints. Within a four square block area, we have 300 break and enters a day, one of Chicago's finest commented, as he sprinkled white powder over the crime scene. I wasn't sure if that statistic was supposed to make me feel less special, or if he was saying welcome to the big city.

And then, almost worse than the burglary, my detested neighbor walked in the door. She had dropped by on a few occasions ostensibly for the proverbial cup of sugar, but her grilling intrusiveness suggested she was some kind of government informant on a covert operation. *Just tell her we're diabetics the next time she comes looking for a cup of sugar,* I had told Carri, *don't let the busybody in.* Now Torquemada was standing in the middle of the crime scene, her head swiveling, eyeballs spinning as though she was on an intelligence gathering mission.

"Whoa, this place is a real mess," she announced, as she sauntered around assessing the disaster. "Looks like you girls got wild and crazy in here."

"No, a junkie dropped by today," I said.

"Well, he probably wanted to surprise you with a home-cooked meal. The kitchen sink is filled with dirty pots and pans. Then again, maybe he was starving after his futile search for valuables." Unable to go for her throat due to the presence of the evidence technicians, I replied in my best Eliza Doolittle voice, "Oh, Darling, those dishes are from a dinner party we had last summer. Now, if you'll excuse me, I must ask you to leave so I can inventory our loss."

Carri came up the stairs just as I was hustling the yenta out the door.

"Don't get scared, Carri, everything is okay, but we were robbed. My dad is now three for three." Carri surveyed the living room then dashed to her bedroom.

"Oh, no, the bastard stole my opal ring, my birthstone!" she wailed. "Oh, god, he got my add-a-pearl necklace too."

"Don't feel bad," I said, "he got my Confirmation watch and my grandmother's cameo."

"Well, ladies," the detective interrupted, "we've done about all we can do here. We got a few prints, but they're probably yours," he laughed. "Doesn't really matter though, we never catch anybody anyway. We dust just to make the victims feel better."

"Makes them think we're on top of things," the other Dick Tracy chuckled, as they beat it out the door.

It was getting late, the circus was over, even Helmet and Mr. Hormet had gotten bored and left. Carri and I cleared a space on the sofa to commiserate.

"He cut the cord on my Princess phone," Carri grieved.

"He got my debate medals." I said, "Let's call it a day. We can clean this dump over the weekend."

"How can we live this way for three days?" Carri yawned.

"We've lived this way since we moved in," I said only half-exaggerating, "except for the time your mother visited. By the way, I'm sleeping on the floor in your room. My bedroom door doesn't lock."

"The floor in my room?"

"Yes, I'm sleeping on your floor in case the creep comes back tonight for something he couldn't carry. My father said criminals often return to the scene of the crime."

"Your father's not infallible. He said guys would be hitting on you, and that hasn't happened. Are you thinking the dope fiend will come back for your class ring?"

"Actually I do – he might come back for more stuff. Your add-a-pearl necklace only had seven pearls, remember?"

"I know I got it when I was born, but then my sister came along and my mother got too busy to order pearls," she said, turning out the light, as I nested on the floor in my down quilt.

"Carri," I murmured in the dark. "I'm sorry about your necklace."

"Don't worry about it," she said. "Someday we'll have diamonds that will dazzle even that bitch upstairs."

The room fell silent as I visualized my drop-dead engagement ring. Then in a soft voice, as though Miss J. Edgar Hoover might be listening, Thing One asked, "Thing Two, how did you realize that the apartment had been ransacked?"

"Well, my bike was gone," I whispered. "It was chained to the radiator in the living room, and I noticed it was missing."

Crash Course

Where did I come from – how did I get here? No one agreed.

My brother said the stork brought you.

My girlfriend said fairies deliver babies.

The girl upstairs said babies are left on doorsteps.

My cousin told me doctors carried dead babies in their black bags and a mother breathes into a baby's nose until it starts to breathe on its own.

Raphaella Caradiso, my fifth-grade best friend, told me she saw some weird looking babies in glass jars at the Museum of Science and Industry.

"Raphy," I said, "That is so stupid. Babies do not come in glass jars."

"Well, I went to the Museum's Chick Hatchery, and I saw with my own eyes baby chickens pop out of eggs. If a chick can crack out of an egg, why can't a baby come packed in a jar?"

Maybe she's right I thought. Everyone says I look like my dad. Maybe my mother picked my jar because I reminded her of my father.

"That makes sense, Raphy, but you're forgetting one thing. Mothers get babies from hospitals not museums."

"Not always," Raphaella countered. "You heard Sister Praxeda tell the Christmas story about the stable, and you saw the Nativity play where Jesus was packed in straw. They didn't show how He got in the manger in the first place."

"None of this makes sense," I admitted. "They say Mary and Joseph left Nazareth on a donkey and she was great with child. I think they meant she was great with children."

"Oh, who knows. Big people lie a lot. Santa Claus turned out to be a big fat fake," Raphy fumed. "Our apartment doesn't even have a stupid chimney and we still get presents."

"You're not saying Jesus was a fake?"

"Of course not, but I do wonder what exactly they're talking about when I hear the Christmas story. What are swaddling clothes? What's a virgin? Was Joseph the father or wasn't he?"

"Well, he was Mary's husband so he had to be the father."

"Don't be so sure. God is Jesus' father. And you know what else? I think the Three Kings, The Magi and the Wise Guys are all the same people."

"They are the same, and they're Wise Men not Wise Guys, but they're weren't that smart if they brought frankincense and myrrh to Baby Jesus instead of a toy. And we're not that smart if we can't even figure out how you get a baby."

"I know," Raphaella lamented. "My mother said I should always come to her if I have any questions, but when I asked where babies came from, she blew her cork. She said, 'I'll tell you when you need to know. I'll tell you when the time is right.' In my house, that means never."

I was too embarrassed to tell Raphy how asking about babies almost got me killed.

Once during a family drive, my mother mentioned to my dad that a cousin was "expecting."

Piping up from the backseat, I asked, "When is she due?" I was about eight years old and had no idea what that meant, but I'd heard a neighbor ask that of a pregnant lady, and I thought it sounded grown-up.

"When is she due?" my father shouted as he practically ran our car off the road and screeched to a halt. "Mary," he thundered, "what are you teaching this kid? Where did she learn that? Who is she talking to," he continued bellowing. "You're not watching her friends," he accused. "You need to talk to her teachers! This kid is out of control."

The virulent tongue-lashing almost had my mother in tears and I definitely got the message that baby talk was taboo. Thanks to fear and shame, I remained ignorant for a very long time, but I vowed that someday when I became a mother, no question would go unanswered and no subject would be off limits.

One day, when my daughter was about seven, I found her and her friend, Cara, playing with their beloved Barbies. There were about a dozen of the stupid strumpets swimming in the Barbie pool with a few boyfriend Kens floating around too. One Barbie/Ken caught my eye.

"Lia," I asked, "what's with Ken's head on Barbie's body?"

"Oh, that's Barbie's gay friend," she chirped. "They're going for a swim before they go shopping."

Her grandfather would have caused a major pile-up.

*... when it first walks into his grave little head
that adults do not always have divine intelligence,
that their judgements are not always wise,
their thinking true, their sentences just – his world
falls into panic desolation. The gods are fallen ...*

— John Steinbeck

Trust Me

This is to certify that

Scalise, Mary Louise

*has completed the work
required by the kindergarten of*

SAINT JEROME SCHOOL

*and is entitled to receive this
Diploma*

Rev. Ferdinand Stahr, O.F.M.
Pastor

Sister M. Cecilia
Principal

Sister Mary Lucille
Teacher

Babies. I hated babies, and here I was on my first day of kindergarten having to hold hands with the five-year-old the baby, Nancy. As we walked, I asked if she'd gotten the small box of Crayolas or the medium box. My mother had assured me that the giant box of Crayolas could only be purchased when you went to first grade. I suspected that my mother didn't want to buy me the giant box as I knew you did most of your coloring in kindergarten and, as you moved to first and second grade, you colored less and less because you had to learn more and more. My brother told me that by the time he got to third grade he barely had any time for coloring so I figured start out with the giant box of Crayolas and work your way down to the smaller size. Then out of nowhere, Nancy started to sob.

"What's the matter?" I asked, afraid that her mother had hadn't bought her any crayons at all. "Don't cry. I got the medium box. You can share my Crayolas – just don't press too hard and smash the tips. I like my crayons to stay sharp and pointy."

53

"I have cwayons," she whimpered, "I'm cwying betuz I don't wanna go to coo."

Cwayons? Betuz? Coo?

Nancy I tried to reassure her, "Don't worry school will be fun. We're going to learn to read; we're going to make paper chains that will fit around the world, we're going to church with the big kids every day . . ."

Suddenly her crying escalated to screaming as some birds landed in the gutter.

"Gooli, gooli," she shrieked, "Gooli, gooli!"

Her mother raced from behind.

"It's okay, Nancy. It's okay, baby! Don't be afraid of the birdies. They won't hurt you!"

As Nancy's mom calmed her down, I ran back to my mother. "Mom, I don't think kindergarten is for me. It's going to be filled with a lot of stupid kids!"

My mother, who had long-awaited the day school would take her middle headache, bent down and whispered in my ear. "You're going to love school! Trust me! I'm the one stuck with a baby at home. You'll be with the big kids saying the Pledge of Allegiance everyday!"

The Pledge of Allegiance was her trump card. Ever since my brother had taught me the Pledge, I had put my hand over my heart and recited it at the site of every American flag.

"You're just saying that because you know I like to pledge, but you can't trick me! Nancy is going to be in my room and she can't even talk! She says *betuz* and *cwying*. She's afraid of pigeons," I shouted, stamping one of my patent-leather Mary Janes. "I am not going to school with babies!"

"Wait one little minute, Miss Bossy! Don't stamp your foot at me. People are staring at us! They think you're the scaredy cat."

The scaredy cat tactic worked. Slowly I began budging my Mary Janes as my mom maneuvered me through the opening day crowd toward the three-flat building St. Jerome's had purchased to handle the explosion of post-World War II progeny. Kindergarten classes were held in the first floor apartment.

Thus began my academic career where I met kids who couldn't even tie their shoes, zipper their jackets or blow their own noses. I was always having to ask some sniffly kid to, "Please wipe your nose on your sleeve because your mucus is disgusting."

Sister Lucille, the post-menopausal harridan, would tell me to mind my own business, but that was because she got to sit at her desk and not at the coloring table watching noses drip green snot while their owners flicked their tongues like windshield wipers swishing the mucus back and forth. Not a day went by that I didn't tell my friend, Frank Girometti, a really smart boy, that these kids made me want to puke. He said they turned his stomach too, but there was nothing we could do about it.

Thank God for Frank's wisdom. Even though he was a boy, he made the days in the apartment bearable.

In the kitchen, we learned ABC's. In one bedroom, we colored and pasted. In the other bedroom, we did our numbers. And in the living room, well, the living room was reserved for God. A giant picture of Jesus' bleeding heart with little flames shooting out of the top and staring eyeballs peeking out from the fire gazed down on the fifty of us as we memorized our prayers.

Initially Sister's desk was in God's room, but some goof kept plugging up the sink in the kitchen so she moved. She probably figured that she didn't need to watch us in the living room anyway since we wouldn't dare misbehave knowing God's bionic eyeballs saw our every move, but she was wrong about that. Despite Jesus' constant surveillance, there were still some mini-pagan types who regularly destroyed the living room, and then claimed that the Devil did it.

Teachers' aides and retirement were unheard of in the Catholic schools. As nuns reached the golden age of dementia and could no longer slap around the big kids, they were demoted to the lower grades, making the partially deaf, grizzled witches the perfect kindergarten drones. The average class size in our school was fifty. There were no parent volunteers to assist. In the late 50's, moms were busy cranking out babies, serving Jell-O molds and ironing sheets and pillowcases.

Frank and I were appointed teacher's helpers which meant we got to run errands, fetch the pastor when things got out of control, grade papers and tidy up the apartment. We deputized a few other kindergartners, and our posse tutored and tested thereby freeing Sister Lucille to indulge in her almost daily nervous breakdowns. She said that God would give Frank and me special seats in heaven, that we were her stars.

So it was fitting that Frank's star and mine would flame out at the same time, though I, being female bore the greater disgrace.

That fateful snowy day, the behavior of the fifty little beasts, as Sister referred to us, was beyond the pale. She threatened to leave if we didn't settle down, but this was a common threat, and she never really walked out. This time, though, she must've needed a little liquid courage to settle her nerves because she really did abandon ship.

She beat it out the door so fast she almost lost her veil in the door jamb. Bedlam erupted. Forty-eight babies started howling. Only Frank and I kept our cool.

"I don't think she's coming back," I yelled to Frank. "She seemed pretty mad this time."

"Well, I'm not waiting for her," he shouted, "I'm leaving."

"We can't just walk out on these screaming mimis," I said.

"Okay," said Frank, "let's all leave!"

Whereupon we announced that when everyone stopped crying, we were going home. The blubbering subsided, and the arduous task of dressing the forty-eight nincompoops began. "Don't worry about getting the right foot into the right boot. It doesn't matter if you walk funny," I instructed as I zippered and buttoned.

"Get in a straight line," Frank ordered, "and stop sniveling or you're staying here alone."

Suddenly Frank pulled me into a corner. "Johnny Boy Colletti just told me he doesn't know where he lives! Probably most of these Howdy Doody heads don't even know which way to go home."

This was exactly the kind of stupidity that drove me nuts. "I'll take care of this, Frank. Trust me."

I ran back to the kitchen. "Okay, everybody, stop the noise and listen to me. I'm going to say a prayer, and you all need to say it after me."

"Dear Jesus, please get us home safely."

"Deaw Jesus, pwease get us home safewy."

"If I live by Pecco's, I will follow Frankie. If I live by Tootie's, I will follow Mary Lou. Amen."

It worked like magic. Pecco's was a store south of school that sold penny candy so everyone knew where it was, and Tootie's, where we also loaded up on licorice during recess, was in the opposite direction. Like a well-rehearsed evacuation plan, we streamed out of the apartment parting like the Red Sea. Frank told me later that he felt like Moses.

I felt like a fourth grade patrol girl as I stood in the middle of 28th Street holding up traffic while the little refugees streamed across. Just as the kids reached the curb on the other side, one of my deputies yelled, "Here comes Sister!" and sure enough this giant black bat came shrieking down the street, "Get back here! Get back here! Turn around right now!" My little army of brain-dead soldiers immediately deserted. I had no choice but to return.

It took a while to unbutton and unzip the ungrateful deserters and take roll-call to be sure we hadn't lost anyone.

Then the Inquisition began.

"Okay," bellowed Sister Lucifer, as the big kids referred to her, "I think I already know the answer to this question, but I want Jesus to hear the answer too. Whose idea was it to leave the kitchen?"

Immediately this little fat turn-coat, whom I had personally helped out of numerous jams, jumped up and fingered Frank and me. "Him, Sistew, and hew too!" And as if that wasn't enough, Pinocchio proceeded to tell the biggest lie I had ever heard in my entire life.

"She told us she was taking us to Tootie's for candy, and Frank was taking the other kids to Pecco's!"

My mouth fell open at the brazenness of this total untruth. I thought Jesus' eyeballs were going to fall right out of the flames, but Jesus didn't even flinch. I knew how He must have felt when the soldiers came for

Him and His number one apostle Peter said, "I don't know this Guy. I never even saw Him in my life!"

She started in on Frank.

"You rotten little boy! Who do you think you are? Where did you think you were going?" Her breathing sounded like Mr. Gianfrosso's when he had a heart attack in his front yard while tying up his tomato plants.

Suddenly she turned her venomous, spitty tongue on me.

"And you! You are the worst! Are-you-really-a-girl?"

Hearing this, all of the little Alger Hisses came running into the kitchen, their eyes as big as garbage can lids, but Sister was too into her feeding frenzy to even notice. "I can understand a boy doing something like this, but a girl? You could have gotten someone killed! You can't be a girl!"

I was rolling my eyeballs thinking she had a lot of nerve wondering if I was a girl. She was the one who wore giant black men's shoes. She even had a mustache. I told my mother about it, but she said, if I ever dared mention Sister's hairy lip, she would break my neck so I kept my mouth shut.

"No real girl would act this way!"

With this, she closed her eyes and put her veiled head down on the desk.

Suddenly the room was very quiet. One of the little dunderheads whined, "Is she dead?"

"No, I'm not dead!" she snarled, as her head flew up, and the horde of mice skittered back to their worksheets.

Having taken a breather, Sister returned to finish off her prey.

"You make me sick," she screamed at me. "You're not a real girl." Her voice trailed off, she was almost crying. "You could never be a nun." Then in a really creepy way, like Gullam addressing a Hobbit, she spewed, "No one would want you."

But Sister couldn't scare me. Instead, I felt sorry for her. Something very bad must have happened to her that she didn't even know a girl when she was looking at one.

"Sister," I said, "Don't worry. I am a girl. I'm named after my Nonna, and I wear dresses with bows. Do you think if I was a boy I'd go to the lavatory with the girls?"

But she just stared up at the Cross, and looked very sad.

"Really, Sister, I'm a girl for sure. I play with dolls and I think boys are stupid," I said. "I don't think it's a bad thing to be a girl. My brother said girls just need to be on guard so no one tries to push them around, and trust me, I will never let that happen."

Not a Permanent Solution

I wonder if, in the Land of Make Believe, these baby dolls have flashbacks about their first permanent wave. Mine was seared into my brain. I was about to start first grade, and neither the nightly ritual of winding endless banana curls nor my non-stop whining about boys yanking on my braids was appealing to my mother. Her beautician cousin Della's suggestion of a hot perm seemed like the perfect solution.

Though I viewed the horrendous contraption with its black wire tentacles and gleaming steel curler clamps with great trepidation, my mom said I'd be too busy reading books to waste time on the nightly hair-setting ritual. This permanent, she promised, would end my hairy tales of woe; I'd be permanently beautiful.

It took hours to section my massive mane into appropriate sized chunks for the electric curlers. Only the promise of a fuchsia hair ribbon forced me to sit still atop two giant Chicago telephone directories. Finally a disgusting permanent wave solution was applied to each curler and Della threw the switch.

Immediately my head started hissing and steaming like a pot of boiling ravioli. With her eyes as big as the giant meatballs my Nonna fried on Sunday morning, my mother asked, "Della, is her head supposed to smoke like that?"

"That's only steam," said Della, "If her hair was burning, we'd smell it – singed hair smells disgusting."

Looking at my mother's popping eyeballs and smelling the stinking fumes sent me into orbit. My sotto sobs erupted into what would have been hair raising shrieks had not my head been so wired.

"This is an electric chair!" I screamed. "I'm turning into Frankenstein!"

My mother grabbed the telephone book highchair.

"Sit still," she hissed. "If you fall off those phone books, you'll be scalped like an Indian and you'll have to wear a babuschka to school. Besides," she grinned, "You told me you wanted to be beautiful!"

That was true. I did want to be beautiful. I settled down.

A few minutes later the wires were disconnected, the hair unwound and a nauseating "neutralizer" was sloshed through my ringlets. Then my locks were twisted into pin curls and I was placed under a giant steel helmet for another hour to dry.

At last my tresses were combed out with the coveted fuchsia bow planted in the massive eagle's nest of curls.

I was beautiful.

Two weeks later my hair was stick straight. The beauty maven said the "hot wave" didn't take; she would give me a "cold wave."

"No, no," I told my mother, "No, more torture. I'll just be me with straight hair. Being beautiful is way too much trouble."

None of My Business

"Why isn't Grandpa buried here?" I asked as I knelt at the family plot. "Why is he at Oak Ridge Cemetery which isn't even Catholic?"

"You're supposed to be praying for the dead not asking nosy questions that are none of your business," my father said, in his usual *you are such a pain in the neck* voice, as he tried to shimmy the old gravestone the years had pushed off center.

"Mom, why doesn't Dad talk to his brother?" I wondered, after sensing that a Maginot Line separated relatives at opposite ends of a wedding reception.

"You don't need to be concerned about that," she answered, staring straight ahead.

"Why do colored kids go to Ward School, and only white kids go to St. Jerome's?" I asked as the public school kids walked past our house on their way to class.

"I suppose because they're not Catholic," my mother said in a tone of voice that suggested I could be on my hands and knees helping her wax the kitchen floor instead of staring out the venetian blinds.

I ignored the hint. "Aren't they worried about going to Hell?"

"I guess not. Go clean your room."

"What's in a CONDEMNED RATED movie that makes it bad?" I asked my friend as we searched the Motion Picture Ratings in the *New World*, hoping to find a Catholic approved movie our parents would let us see.

"*Baby Doll* is a dirty movie that's why it's a C," Margie confided, "but we're not supposed to be talking about that stuff. Don't even look at the CONDEMNED's," she cautioned.

After years of "don't be so nosy" and "mind your own business," I realized I'd probably never know why my mother's brother lived in a hospital, what disease killed my favorite uncle or why colored people lived two blocks away, but never crossed the great divide of Wentworth Avenue. Silence, oblique answers, tidbits of information and terse responses frustrated even my most crucial queries: "Did Grandpa leave behind a wife in Italy?"

Years later, I could relate to the rabbi who prayed at the Wailing Wall for a half century with no reward. "What does it feel like to pray for peace at the Wailing Wall for fifty years only to have your country in constant conflict?" he was asked.

"It feels like I'm talking to a fucking wall," he said.

I sympathized, but at least he'd never been subjected to the Sister Adorers of the Most Precious Blood, human stones, who viewed questions as treason, and did graduate work in stonewalling.

Long before learning to read books, I learned to read people thanks to my family members and their volcanic temperaments. When not shouting, they used body language and facial expressions to suppress any curiosity regarding what seemed implausible if not downright impossible. Glaring eyes, exasperated sighs, glances of disapproval, the phonics of dysfunction, enabled me to decode the language of concealment.

The list of verboten topics encompassed everything from family history to current events, and was complicated by the fact that no map existed showing where the land mines lay. An innocuous inquiry could detonate an explosion of confusion that neither education nor therapy could heal.

"Sister, why would God punish a baby and send it to Limbo forever just because she died before she was baptized?"

"God knows what is best," Sister said.

"Sister," I'd try again when the waters seemed calm, "if your body must be buried in a consecrated cemetery in order to go to heaven, what happens to people who burn in fires? What happens if someone dies in the forest and an animal eats him? Does he go to hell?"

"Finish your assignment, the animals in the forest don't take spelling tests."

"Sister," I'd try again, "what happened to the Roman martyrs who were eaten alive by the lions in the Coliseum? What if lions left an arm or a leg? Would the arm and leg get buried? Would just the arm and leg go to heaven? Would God say, 'I'm omniscient so I know who you are even without your head. Come on in?'"

"You are making Jesus very sad with your silly questions."

I couldn't stop wondering and worrying, not just about the Coliseum and the Limbo babies, but also about my friend Catherine's mother who was getting divorced and going to Hell. Catherine said her mother told her it was better to go to Hell than stay married to her father. How could anyone deliberately antagonize God with a statement like that? I could just hear God saying, "That's it, Lady, you're toast!" I was terrified for her, and sad for Catherine to have a mother with one foot on a banana peel to Hell.

And then there was Raymond from across the street who was killed in a car crash the very same Sunday he slept through Mass, a mortal sin. All the busybodies said his mother set the alarm clock for him, but he turned it off. Did he turn it off intentionally and say, "I don't feel like going to Mass today," or did he turn it off thinking he'd just lay there for an extra five minutes, and accidentally fall back to sleep? One way he'd burn for eternity, but, if it was an accident, Sister said God would show mercy and, after the lazybones did a little time in Purgatory to make up for being a slug, he'd fly up to Heaven.

I started to think there was something wrong with me, that I was supposed to stop with the questions, and mind my own business. Could it be that there were things I wasn't supposed to understand; maybe it was true that if I was supposed to know, they'd tell me.

I asked about it in Confession, but the priest just said, "Bless you, my child, just believe." He didn't get it; I wanted to believe, but there were a lot of things that just weren't adding up, and, as time passed, there were more inconsistencies, contradictions and even some big fat lies.

Why did priests drive luxury cars that they traded in every year while the nuns lived in poverty?

Why did indulgences vanish, and what happened to exorcism?

Why were rich people given annulments, and those without resources excommunicated?

And when it came to abortion, I pictured God standing at the Pearly Gates with a calendar. "Okay, this woman had an abortion in the 16th century when the Church had no problem with abortion so she can come in, but this lady had one after we changed the rules, so sad, too bad." Was God really that cruel?

What happened to 4 million dollars that vanished from the coffers of the Council of Bishops when Chicago's Cardinal was treasurer, and why did his divorced cousin and her sons live within a block of him no matter where he was assigned?

From the ridiculous to the scandalous, the questions piled up.

Cardinal George one day called a press conference to announce that the Pope had declared Limbo, that holding pen for unbaptized babies, a thing of the past. "From now on," he proclaimed, "Limbo will no longer be taught."

"Does that mean," an obviously pagan reporter had the nerve to ask, "that Limbo *no longer exists*?"

"I didn't say that," said the tap-dancing leader of the flock, "I said the papal directive states that it will *no longer be taught*." Whoa, how's that for parsing, President Clinton?

But some papal pronouncements are clearer and, while the faithful may ignore them, there are always a few sharpies who take exception.

"In the interests of unity in the Church . . ." the Pope recently UN-excommunicated a bishop who loudly proclaims that no Jews were gassed in the Nazi death camps. After a disastrous two weeks of international outrage, the Pope backpedaled insisting that no one had told him, the *German* Pontiff, about this hatemonger's infamous reputation.

Maybe the Pope should have asked a few questions like what's a Holocaust denier. Maybe he should have asked about hypocrisy. Or what is complicity? If he's persistent, he might even get around to asking about pedophilia.

On second thought, he might not want to make Jesus cry.

No Surprises

"Park your car, Doc! Right here, Doc! Park your car, Doc!"

Those sing-song words meant the White Sox were playing at Comiskey Park, and my brother and his buddies were making money.

Never being included in the action bothered me so I went to whine to my dad who was tuned to his transistor radio.

"Dad," I asked, "Anthony gets an allowance like me so why is he parking cars for money?"

"It's always better to make your own money," he answered. "Then you can be independent and take care of yourself."

"When I get bigger, I'm going to park cars and make money to take care of you and mom."

"Girls can't park cars," he said, just as Bob Elson announced strike three with the Sox on top. "It's harder for women to make money because there are a lot of jobs they can't do."

"So you give me an allowance forever?"

"No, it means that someday you'll marry a man who'll take care of you, and you'll get a good education just in case something happens to him."

"What if I can't find a man who wants me," I worried, thinking about old maid Angelina down the street.

"That's why you need an education to fall back on so you can be independent, and take care of yourself. Go play with your sister. The Sox are up to bat," he said, as he turned his attention back to the game.

Did he just say that I could only be independent if something happened to my husband or if I didn't get married? If you were someone's wife, you couldn't be independent? But what if my husband said I could be independent?

I had more questions, but I knew better than to keep bugging Dad when he was listening to baseball. Why couldn't girls park cars? Why were the boys telling men where to park when they didn't even own the street? What if a husband didn't want to take care of his wife, if he was stingy or mean? What if she didn't like the way he was taking care of her?

There was no asking my brother. He'd tell me to quit sticking my nose where it didn't belong. Besides, even though boys thought they knew it all, they really didn't. He probably wouldn't know why it was harder for women to make money or how I could find a rich man to take care of me.

Luckily I had a good brain. Even my brother said I was smart for a girl. I'd go to college just in case no one wanted to marry me. And if no one wanted to marry me, that wouldn't be so terrible; boys didn't impress me. I mean, God didn't even trust them to have babies. If I stayed on the honor roll, maybe I could even skip the marriage part, and jump right into taking care of myself. Who decided a husband should be in charge of a wife? It seemed to me that if two smart people married that could spell trouble. Why would a woman agree to this set-up?

My dad handed over his paycheck to my mom every Friday, but it wasn't really hers. She didn't go to work every day and earn it. I almost never saw her buy anything for herself. Did she think it was a good deal not to have a job and just cook, clean, mop, sew, bake, grocery shop, wash windows, iron, do laundry, scrub floors, take care of us kids, drag around the Electro-Lux and drink coffee? Was she glad she didn't drive, and that Daddy took her everywhere that was too far to walk?

I wondered if she liked being told what to do, if she was happy being taken care of. It seemed like if someone took care of you, you had to do what they wanted; they got to boss you around. My dad told my mom after they got married that she no longer needed friends because now she had a husband. Was it easier to let someone else make all the decisions?

She wanted to move out of the old neighborhood, but when she'd say *let's buy a house*, he'd say, "Mary, now is not the time. We've got three kids to put through college." Couldn't they vote on some things? But voting wasn't the answer because it would be a tie, and you just know, he'd be the tie-breaker. Sometimes mom would speak up, and say what was on her mind, but she really couldn't change anything except maybe the color of our bedroom.

Sister said the Golden Rule was *Do unto others, as you would have them do unto you*, but JoAnn's father said it really was "He who has the gold, rules." I didn't intend to rule anybody and I didn't care about being rich; independence sounded like the way to go. One day I made a list of rules, rules that would make me my own boss.

1. Go to college.
2. Drive a car.
3. Get a good job.
4. Save my money.
5. Dye my hair.
6. Smoke cigarettes.
7. Wear lipstick.
8. Buy myself presents.
9. Make my own decisions.
10. Marry a smart man.

I found my Mother in the kitchen slaving over the ironing board. "Mom," I asked, "could you read these rules, and tell me what you think; they're for when I grow up."

She put the iron on its triangle resting plate. Her first *hmmm* as she read sounded like she was thinking *okay, not bad,* but as she neared the bottom of the page, her *hmmm* sounded like *really now, is that so?"*

She was quiet for a minute as she placed my notebook on the table, and resumed chasing wrinkles. Finally she shook her head and gave me one of those what-am-I-going-to-do-with-you smiles.

"What you wrote is very interesting. In fact, the first four ideas are excellent, but I thought you hated rules."

"I don't hate all rules, just stupid rules, like only taking ten books out of the library at one time. My rules are different."

"So you decide which rules are stupid, and which are important?"

"Why not? Why would I want to follow someone else's rules?" I questioned. "Didn't you read number nine? I'll make my own decisions." I refrained from adding *And I already decided that ironing is a waste of time.* "Now I have to do what I'm told, but, boy, when I grow up I'm not going to listen to anyone but me. Before I get married, I'm going to tell my boyfriend that if he thinks he's going to be my boss, we better not get married."

She blew over the marriage part, probably thinking *Sweetie, you're going to be left on the vine forever* and said, "Going to college, getting a good job and saving money will help you take charge of your own life, but why on earth would you want to smoke cigarettes and dye your hair?"

I didn't want to hurt her feelings and tell her that Red-Headed Ann, a woman who lived on the next block, smoked Viceroys, dyed her hair red-orange and drove a fancy car, always looked like she was having fun. I didn't want to confess that not only did I plan to be independent, but I intended to be glamorous too. I knew Red-Headed Ann would never waste a minute polishing doorknobs when she could have been out cruising the neighborhood.

As if reading my mind, while maneuvering the hot metal tip of the iron into the corner of my father's shirt sleeve, mom said, "You probably think smoking and dyed hair are glamorous because that's what you see in magazines, but smoking is bad for your lungs, and hair dye turns your hair to straw." Then, holding the iron down on the shirt for so long I thought she was going to scorch it, she added, "You have a lot to learn, Missy."

She flashed a weird smile. "Just wait and see what happens when you fall in love and get married, Miss Smarty Pants."

I knew by the way she enunciated *Miss Smarty Pants* that she meant *she'll find out someday, she'll change her tune.*

"Well, this much I know for sure. I'm going to pick my own friends, and pay my own bills. and be free."

"Even with a plan, life doesn't always go your way," she said, "Sometimes you get surprises."

I wondered if she'd had a plan that got goofed up when she got married. I wanted to ask, but I thought she might feel bad if that was what had happened. The thought of that made me very sad so, for once, I shut up.

She snatched a blouse from the laundry basket, and sprayed some starch on the collar. I took my notebook and started scribbling.

"Changing your rules already?" she asked.

"Nope, just adding eleven and twelve. *Don't let anyone change my plan,* and *No surprises.*"

The Sleeping Baby

Girls didn't get kicked out of school.

Even boys didn't get kicked out of school unless they were totally incorrigible, and incorrigible was loosely defined.

Bean the Fiend practically killed someone with a baseball bat, and he didn't even get suspended. They said it was because the guy he almost murdered was colored, and colored people were not supposed to come into Bridgeport so he was really asking for it. But my dad said no human being deserved such treatment, and the incident was a dirty shame. Nothing happened to Bean and he should have been history.

Joey the Nut torched someone's garage: he wasn't expelled either. The grapevine had it that graduation was only a couple of weeks away so the nuns didn't want to bother, but I suspected they were worried the convent would go up in flames if they dared get rid of him.

Two criminals skated, and the nuns wanted to throw me out?

The day before, Sister Margaret Anne, my six foot, seventh grade teacher, who sported more than a bit of a mustache, had clomped over to my desk in her huge black wing-tips and handed me an envelope. "Give

75

this to your parents," she barked. "I want to see them as soon as possible."

In the days before teacher conferences were routine, when dads worked double shifts, when moms made tri-colored Jell-O molds and baked cookies from scratch, having your mother, never mind both parents, called to school was equivalent to an executioner's drum roll.

I sat at the kitchen table preparing myself for something awful, but this?

"You finally did it," my father announced as he hung up his jacket and pulled out a chair at the table. He and my mother had just returned from the dreaded meeting. "You got yourself thrown out." Lowering his voice so as not to wake my sister, he continued, "Yes, the nuns have finally had enough of your big mouth. They want you gone – out of there – by the end of the school year. Shaking his head and raising his eyebrows with a you-just-never-learn look, he added, "I've told you a million times to watch your step."

"Jim, stop it," my mother said as she put away cooking utensils. I could not believe mom was fooling around putting away the dinner dishes at a time like this. Apparently she'd yet to realize my disgrace would instantly qualify her for The Mothers Who Failed Hall of Shame.

My heart was thumping; I thought my pajama top would fly up in my face. I knew my father was not joking because he had almost no sense of humor plus he had warned me, "Your smart mouth will get you in trouble one day. Mark my words." It was clear that a girl who spoke out had a major disability. Sooner or later, she was guaranteed her Waterloo.

But it seemed so drastic.

True, I had gotten more than my share of checkmarks in kindergarten, but, for the most part, I had cleaned up my act. Gone was the girl who would not put her head down on her desk and rest quietly, wait her turn patiently at lavatory time or play well with others. I still had a few flaws, but not enough to warrant capital punishment. My grades were excellent. I'd read my brother's copy of *All Quiet on the Western Front* by the time I was ten. I wasn't perfect, but, unlike a lot of the troublemakers in my room, I never had to put money in the Mission Box for The Pagan Babies in China.

Okay, so I finished my assignments lickety-split and passed notes until the slow-pokes were done with their work. But I was also the one who helped other kids diagram sentences and drilled them on the state capitals. This was my thank-you for grading all of Sister's spelling tests every week, for putting all the arithmetic problems on the blackboard every morning? This was my reward for spending my daily recess down in first grade dressing the brats who couldn't even tell their right boot from their left? Would they really dump their star funeral mass singer who chanted countless dirges whenever another parishioner kicked the bucket?

My mother, noting the shock waves of disbelief and anger roll across my face, intervened.

"Jim, stop this nonsense," she insisted, "tell her the truth." My mom was trying to pull me in off the ledge my father was greasing.

As she stood at the sink filling Skippy's water bowl, she said, "You are being double promoted because of some test your class took. Your scores were high."

"You don't really believe that, do you, Mary?" my dad interrupted. "She's a giant pain and they want her out of their hair."

Just before the meeting, my mother had taken a cake out of the oven and now she put it on the table. She believed food always made things better.

"Yes, they're sick of putting up with her," he said, while I sat there totally bewildered. "Sister didn't want to be blunt, but I could read between the lines. She was trying to be nice."

"No, that's not true," my mother shot back, cutting an extra big piece of chocolate cake for me. "Daddy's just saying that because he doesn't want you to think *who you are*." He doesn't want you to get a big head," she added, as though this all made perfect sense.

Was my father practicing his version of that old Italian adage about only kissing sleeping babies? If you kissed a baby when she was awake she might think she was really special, really important, and, God forbid, think *who she was.*

Sensing my confusion and getting impatient with this mind-game, my mother picked up the empty plates and put them in the sink. "Listen to me. Sister Benedict said you need to be challenged. On Monday, you'll go to 8th grade for two months and then graduate. Now get to bed. It's late."

The drama was over, just like that. No one asked if this was something I'd like to do or what did I think. No discussion, just get to bed.

The thumping of my heart subsided, but the spinning in my head had only just begun. The master of mixed messages had added another chapter, *Planting the Seeds of Self-Doubt,* to his best-seller *How to Destroy Your Kid's Confidence.*

For graduation I was given a beautiful wristwatch with a tiny diamond on each corner of its delicate hinged platinum case. The square white-gold face had small, swirly Arabic numerals at 3, 6, 9 and 12. My mother confided that she'd objected to the expense, but my dad told her my present had to be really special to show me how pleased they were with my achievement. Why couldn't he have told me that? Why couldn't he just say, "Your mother and I are really proud of you."

And then it occurred to me that, maybe as a baby, he'd only been kissed when he was sleeping.

Don't We All and Haven't We Always

When I write about my father, the picture painted can be harsh. It was a thorny relationship, I joked, because we were twins born thirty-three years apart – mirror images who shared generous hearts and quick minds, but also iron wills and fierce tempers – a volatile combination. Perhaps a lithograph, where oil and water don't mix, better describes the bond, but I prefer heavy oils which never fade.

Paintings require contrast and balance, emphasis and proportion and perspective. No small task to see a picture when one is in it, distance oneself when love blurs the vision, or appreciate a child's worm's-eye view for what it is – justified, but limited.

The brush of humor blends rough lines, the stroke of wit softens glaring reality but, without perspective, the finished product is one-dimensional, without texture or shape. Creating the illusion of three dimensions by applying layers of heavy oil, scraped from the palette of emotion with tints of laughter and shades of hurt, is no substitute. Though impaired eyesight was corrected early on – I wore eyeglasses from third grade – it would take much longer for me to recognize my heart's limited perception, clouded by circumstance, distorted by pain.

Age, however, changed my vision, allowed me to fly above the landscape, to get a bird's-eye view of a sub-culture which rigidly defined the male role as man of the house, breadwinner, ruler of the roost and king of the castle. A culture that not only accepted certain behaviors, but expected and required them as well. A culture that revered rules, and valued authority over expression – where shame and fear kept people in line – where life was serious, tough, leaving no room for mistakes, risks or wrong moves – where there were no second chances.

New lenses improved my mind-sight. My expanded point of view neither justified nor defended; it simply clarified and validated. And that clarification and validation shifted me toward the light, toward understanding and compassion, allowing me to inch forward.

At that time, in that culture does not excuse the absurd nor rationalize the unacceptable, but it does allow me to see the man behind the behavior, a man who did his best with what he knew. And except for the psychopaths of the world, don't we all and haven't we always?

The mother who had her kid's feet x-rayed in the shoe store to insure a good fit, who cradled her baby in the passenger seat, the parents who told their kids they weren't smart enough, good enough, fill-in-the-blank enough to make them stronger, more resilient to life's vagaries, were acting out of concern and love.

The doctor who prescribed a stiff cocktail for the overwhelmed patient, the experts who advised parents to not talk about the death of a child, to just move on with their lives, the priests who counseled women to stay in abusive marriages believed they were operating in everyone's best interests.

Mistakes made in the name of progress, in the name of honor, in the name of God, in the name of love.

Wearing my *at that time, in that culture* spectacles, I see that long before one is a parent, one is a human being with often too little time, too many demands, too much responsibility and too few resources. I realize some of life's best lessons are about what not to do. I celebrate, through story-telling, the hilarious parts of my experience and I document the painful to weaken its hold.

Most importantly, I no longer evaluate yesterday's mistakes under today's microscope.

I accept that once I know better, I am obligated to do better. I am committed to not repeating errors, to speaking out when my gut tells me something is amiss. And if I miss such an opportunity, I pray my children know I did the best I could and extract every last bit of humor from my less than perfect parenting.

I hope they look back to the past to understand and appreciate, but not get stuck staring. I pray they have the moxie to paint their own pictures and the courage to include a self-portrait.

And finally I trust they will take responsibility for their lives and understand that, after all is said and done, they are the curators of their own collections.

When You See with Your Heart

Shortly after Thanksgiving, my youngest sat on Santa's knee in front of the magnificent Christmas tree at Marshall Field's, and she gave him her not very long wish list – a baby doll, a bicycle and, of course, Barbie.

She had only been in the United States for six months, but Barbie already was her new best friend.

My husband hurried to Carmen's Bike Shop to order her first two-wheeler, in part because he couldn't bear to disappoint her, and also, I suspected, because he feared getting stuck assembling a last minute purchase.

"Please don't buy a Barbie bike," I begged as he headed out. "I'm already Barbie'd out."

"I'll look for a Susan B. Anthony bike," he teased, "with defiant little fists waving from the handlebars."

"I'm serious," I said. "Girls relate to their dolls, and, if Barbie was real she'd be six feet tall, weigh 100 pounds, and wear a 42 FF bra. Lia does not need to be a moving billboard advertising the shameless hussy."

"Oh, stop it. If you feel that way, I'll order a Flying Nun bike," he said, as he kissed me good-bye. "And get shopping before the dazzling damsels disappear from the shelves."

I enlisted my mother for the attack on Toys "R" Us before the hordes invaded. We found the Happy Holiday Barbie, the Stupid Barbie, the Malibu Barbie, the Doctor Barbie – a few of the many little anorexics she just had to have. Taking a deep breath, I tried to select the least offensive of the idols and settled on Veterinarian Barbie and Little Mermaid Barbie. Feminist that I was, I hoped not to run into any friends who might spot the pert-nosed, Aryan femme fatales in my shopping cart.

"Guard the cart with your life," I said to my mother. These Barbies are hot items. I'll track down the baby dolls." Fortunately, the human-looking dolls were not in such high demand. I found two infant dolls – one for Lia and one for her sister, Gianna.

I returned to Nonna who was on guard-duty with the Barbie babes.

"What do you think of these, Mom?" I asked, holding up the baby dolls. "They drink a bottle, pee, and cry. Do you think the girls will like them?"

Nonna looked at the babies. "They're adorable," she said, "look at the eyelashes and little bonnets. They're so lifelike," she marveled, "but, Mar," she smiled, shaking her head, *"they're brown."*

"Ma," I said, "Are you kidding me? My daughters are brown."

"What do you mean, your kids are brown?"

"Mom, my girls are from Colombia. They're not blue-eyed blondes. They have brown skin," I said, incredulous that we were having this genetic refresher course in the middle of Toys "R" Us while, in the next aisle, maniacal parents fought over the last of the Teenage Mutant Turtles.

"Oh my God," said Nonna. "I never thought about it, but you're right."

I'm right?

"Ma, please, you're putting me on, aren't you? I mean, *you have noticed* your adopted granddaughters have dark skin?"

"Well, I guess so," she said. "Now that I think about it, I must have, but I never really paid much attention. I mean, what difference does it make? Who cares?"

Indeed, why would anyone care when you see with your heart.

She's Done

My dad said I had to be a little fish in a big pond in order to grow, that I needed to make some new friends, expand my horizons, leave the old neighborhood and interact with girls whose ambitions transcended beauty school. So I was exiled to a high school that required three bus transfers, a place where I wouldn't know a soul. Study on the bus ride my mother said, learn to navigate the city – like I was supposed to be some kind of Christopher Columbus in search of a new world.

Soon I was trudging to the 26th Street bus, but not before I'd sneak under our porch and ditch the embarrassing book bag and, if it had snowed, the humiliating boots my father insisted I wear. It was bad enough that the nuns required us to wear hideous black crepe-soled shoes so as not to scuff the tiled floors, but I drew the line at the mukluk look.

My new girlfriends could have been my cousins, though their names didn't end in vowels. They were first generation, European progeny who didn't eat meat on Fridays, and worried about going to Hell. I translated Caesar's Gallic Wars with the best of them, and even had a leg up when we studied the Renaissance masters, thanks to my ethnicity. The curriculum on sexuality was limited to the dissection of frogs. A couple of sluts, a new word I added to my expanded vocabulary, gossiped about

French kissing, and one warned me to stay away from lesbians. I thought lesbian was a nonsense word akin to jabberwocky. While many of my new classmates' aspirations were not limited by gender or tradition, the One True Faith, like a great cement ankle bracelet, detoured us from the real world.

Until I met Linda.

My new friend was sweet and funny with a face and figure that made our flying-monkey uniform almost attractive. She lived three parishes away on the other side of a viaduct which separated our neighborhood, the *other side*, as we referred to it, was a smidgen more cosmopolitan, but, thanks to both of us being kept on short leashes at home, we were on equal footing when it came to worldliness – one crepe-sole rooted in parochialism, the other inching toward adventure.

One Monday, a not so exuberant Linda flashed her student pass at the bus driver, and flopped into the seat beside me.

"My life is over," she stage whispered.

"Let me guess. Your dog ate your science project."

"This isn't a joke. I'm done. My life is a disaster."

"What happened? Did you fight with your mother? Are you sick?"

"Worse. I had a horrible date Saturday night." She wiped her eyes with the sleeve of her flying-monkey bolero. "I wish I was dead."

"You're crying over a boy? Are you kidding me?"

"I'm not kidding. He's awful – crude, cocky, crazy-mean, and now I'm his girl. My life is ruined. I should just finish myself off."

"Stop the drama. I don't get it. This was a first date with a jerk who asked you to be his girlfriend?"

"He didn't ask me. He said, 'I been watchin' you, and I like you. You're my girl now – you only date me.' But I can't stand him. He's disgusting, he's not even cute, he gives me the creeps, I'm afraid of him."

"One date, and he thinks he owns you? He's a nut – just tell him to drop dead when he calls, tell him you're not interested."

"Not interested? You don't understand, that's the scary part," she whispered. "He's connected."

"Connected? Connected to what? He's 17-years-old, tell him to get lost, or your dad will kick his butt."

"Lower your voice," she hissed. "You don't get it. My dad can't help me. He'll kill my dad, my mother too – he's a hit guy. He's mobbed up."

"Oh, knock it off. You're being ridiculous – he's seventeen; he's a punk. You can't be a mobster at seventeen," I said. "Don't be afraid, the sicko is just trying to scare you."

The bus pulled up to the curb of our school. Linda was in a daze, and didn't move; the peter-pan collar of her blouse was damp from tears.

"C'mon, Linda, we're here. Let's go. We'll figure this out," I said, as we headed off to translate another chapter of Caesar's Gallic Wars.

That night at dinner, I told my girlfriend's story. "She had one date with this goof, and he thinks he owns her. Did you ever hear of such craziness? She thinks her life is over."

I expected my dad, who was afraid of no one, to say that the guy sounded like a loser, that she should just tell her father. Instead he said, "Eat. Your food is getting cold."

I turned to my brother. "Maybe you know this jerk. His name is Eddie Garren."

"He's a creep," my brother said, "a really bad guy, hazardous to her health."

"Get serious," I scoffed.

"No, you get serious," my father snapped. "Your brother's right, be alert; stay away. She's done."

I found a new route to school. Every now and then, I'd bump into Linda, but I'd keep my distance, avoid her at lunch, always too busy to talk. I knew she understood. We both understood. I had to stay on course; expanding horizons was a full-time job – be alert for bad influences, steer clear of hazards. She knew from that first encounter that she was in trouble – that gossip, loneliness and fear would be her new companions.

I trained for debate and symposiums, joined clubs, concentrated on my GPA. Over time, I settled into the big pond, and even got to be a decent sized fish.

I lost track of Linda, though I'd heard that she'd married the psychopath. Occasionally I'd see the monster's name in the news, but it wasn't as though I was following his career.

Then in December of 1999, Chicago headlines announced that Eddie "the Little Guy" Garren, a reputed top mobster, was shot and critically wounded in the alley behind his home as he headed to the funeral of an underworld associate.

Garren had been released only days before the shooting from federal prison after being sentenced to 25 years for masterminding an armed robbery. At the time of his sentencing, he had been arrested 58 times as an adult and convicted 13 times. He had attained special criminal status under a federal law known as the "Dangerous Special Offender Statute."

He never recovered, and died one month later in January, 2000. His obituary described him as a henchman, master thief, robber, hijacker, ringleader, fence, juice collector and rapist. He was survived by two sons and Linda. A half dozen years later, his eldest, Edward, Jr., testified in Chicago's infamous Family Secrets trial that his father had trained him to follow in his footsteps as a burglar and bookmaker.

She was done from the start.

*The best hope is that one of these days
the ground will get disgusted enough
just to walk away leaving people with
nothing more to stand on than what they have so
bloody well stood for up to now.*

— *Patchen*

Abandon All Hope

The two ten-year-old girls raced in, an hour late for school. Wendy, the brains of the outfit, signaled she was going to launch into the latest episode of "How the World Turns in the Projects." Janell, from her perfect little rosebud lips to her parakeet ankles, exuded a *don't mess with me* attitude.

"Miss S, don't expect me and Janell to do no work today. We was trick-or-treating 'til twelve o'clock last night."

"Twelve o'clock? You were out 'til midnight trick-or-treating?"

"Uh-huh, we was out from after school and was jus' finishin' up when some Kings ripped us off. Tell her, Janell. Our pillowcases was filled to the top and they just grabbed 'em and took off."

"Wendy ain't lyin', Miss S, them bastards got it all 'cept the fuckin' Skittles we was eatin' an' it was pass ten o'clock," Janell testified.

"So you went home without candy?"

"No candy?" Wendy flashed the same you-are-so-stupid look she'd bestowed on me when I told her that third-graders shouldn't wear lipstick. "We got us some garbage bags, Miss S, and started all over again."

"Go to your seats, we're on page forty-seven."

Go-to-your-seats? Two ten-year-old girls had been out on the street past midnight, and I was beyond shock.

To a kid from Catholic school, public schools sounded like mysterious gulags. The nuns' favorite threat, "If you don't behave, you'll be sent to public school . . ." made an impression that went unchallenged until I went off to the University of Illinois and saw firsthand that the parochial system didn't have the corner on education. So when I heard of a special Chicago Board of Education program designed to address a desperate teacher shortage, I applied. While contemplating what to do with my life, I figured I could try to provide kids with a trampoline to a better future.

I agreed to take twelve hours of education classes in night school and, on the spot, received a provisional teaching certificate. Few "provisionals" were there because it was their dream job. The men wanted the Viet Nam draft exemption; the females had visions of LBJ's Great Society and summers off. I joined the ranks because my father had declared that I'd storm Broadway with my Theatre degree over his dead body, and I needed time to determine how I was going to maneuver around the corpse.

We were an odd lot from big cities and small towns – twenty-somethings who hadn't a clue that we were the "ye" Dante meant when he wrote *Abandon all hope, ye who enter here.*

A week long in-service, paid for by Great Society dollars, qualified us to teach. We got the CliffsNotes version of The Psychology of the Inner-City Child, role-played parent-teacher conferences, signed mountains of forms, and had a "you've got a pulse/blood pressure normal" physical.

The last afternoon we were given sensitivity training by a dashiki-clad Reverend who raged about nobody wanting goddamned stupid honkies teaching Black kids. "The best White teacher," he declared, "will never compare to the worst Black Teacher!" Some of us were a bit taken aback by his diatribe, but many of the Ivory recruits admired " . . . his honesty for telling it like it is." I thought the Brother had it partly right, without a doubt, many honkies were stupid.

The Reverend needn't have worried about me invading his no-fly zone. In Chicago, zip codes pretty much determine race, and my assignment's zip was smack in the middle of Latin King turf with a few residents tossed into the mix who'd have belonged to the Klan if they hadn't left Dixie.

In the gangbangers' stomping grounds, I learned what made for a successful provisional teacher. Showing up for work qualified dead men walking as SATISFACTORY. Those who prevented the children from killing each other were labeled GOOD and those who did both were deemed EXCELLENT. If you were a male gym teacher, you were EXCELLENT PLUS.

NO GYM CLASSES TODAY scribbled on the teachers' sign-in sheet was all it took to put Coach in charge of the building while the principal ran off to a Cubs game. Bonding over sports and tales of frat escapades, plus the on-the-job training, guaranteed a man, whose IQ was equal to the final score of a Bears game, a slot on the executive roster. It was no wonder that administrators, who evaluated struggling teachers, were often more incompetent than their quarry. Long before William Bennett, then Secretary of Education, labeled the CPS ". . . the worst school system in the country," pathetic administrators and pitiful teachers were diligently laboring to earn the title.

In fairness, though, they did not destroy public education on their own.

In the 50's, Chicago had the largest parochial school system in the country supported by the city's huge Catholic population which formed a monolithic voting bloc. Since these voters neither used nor cared about the public schools, the Chicago machine decided that the system, a huge drain on the city's coffers, was expendable. The politicians did not intend to eliminate public education, they just didn't want to fund it. There was no grand exit strategy, the powers that be just walked away. And no one blinked. Decades before George Bush's No Child Left Behind Act became law, Chicago implemented the Throw Public School Kids Under the Bus Initiative.

The system never recovered.

Now we provisional teachers, unqualified, untrained and unprepared, were being foisted on an operation that had long been tottering on the edge of a cliff.

The assistant principal assigned classrooms – girls to the lower grades, men to the Upper Grade Center. I was given a "kindofa third/fourth grade class," by Mr. Second-in-Command who, no doubt, yearned for the day when he could play dead in the principal's chair. But he'd have a tough act to follow.

The day after Martin Luther King was killed, Chicago's westside went up in flames. No teacher was to leave early, the principal dictated, but with the action less than three miles away, tension was high. After lunch, when the melee was revving up to a full-blown disaster, but before Mayor Daley's infamous "shoot to kill" order, Captain Courageous chose to jump ship and had Coach drive him home. Unfortunately, Coach drove his convertible straight into the conflagration, where the angry mob tore into the canvas top. Coach was unable to shield our fearless leader from the unruly crowd. The following day word of the incident provided the silver lining in the catastrophic cloud.

But on my first day, I was not privy to the history of dysfunction. I had to hit the ground running which meant inhaling the Chicago Public Schools' curriculum du jour known as Continuous Progress. I was baffled by the concept; in a school setting I assumed continuous progress was a given. I wondered if Stalled Progress and Intermittent Progress had been tried and found wanting.

Continuous Progress was based on a "spiral concept." If a child failed to grasp short vowels, for instance, the teacher proceeded to the next concept. The unlearned material would be repeated somewhere up the spiral as the spiral continued spiraling. I'd yet to take a methods course, but the idea sounded like teaching a student to merge in traffic when he couldn't get the hang of starting the car.

The primary grades were organized in divisions of P1, P2, P3 and PZ. PZ stood for Primary Zero, code for third-graders who could not function in fourth. To protect their self-esteem, PZ was invented.

"So you're the new PZ rookie," the man said when I answered his knock. "Good luck with those morons tomorrow."

"Morons?"

"Yeah, I taught your kids last year. Well, I didn't actually teach them because they're incapable of learning. I tried for months to get them to add, and then finally I thought screw it and moved on to borrowing."

"How did you teach borrowing if they couldn't add?

"Well, I didn't teach borrowing because they couldn't get the hang of that either. They were hung up on place value so I just dropped math and concentrated on science."

"You just ignored math?" I asked, thinking he was pulling the new-bie's leg.

"Yeah, Continuous Progress is great. If you get sick of teaching the idiots the same thing day after day, you just move on to something else. The fucking curriculum spirals."

"John Dewey would've put a gun to his head if he'd ever heard of Continuous Spiraling," I said.

"Speaking of guns, did I tell you I was a cop?"

"A cop? I thought you taught my kids last year."

"Well, I'm a cop too. During the day I teach, and at night I'm a Chicago cop."

"You cannot be serious."

"No, for real. I work the night shift for the CPD."

"You must be wiped out, teaching and holding down a second full-time job with so much stress."

"Nah, I just hide my squad under a viaduct and catch some z's and, when I teach, I mostly sit. Gets a little tricky during tax season 'cause I do taxes too."

"You're quite the Renaissance man," I marveled. "How do you handle discipline? Pull out your gun when the kids act up?"

"Believe me, I feel like it sometime. These kids are wackos," he said. "I'll give you a tip. If a boy acts up just make him wear a babushka, and stand in front of the class the rest of the day. Works like a charm. A little embarassment, and they shape up," he bragged. "Except for one kid, Ricardo – he really loves babushkas. He wants to wear lipstick too. I think he's a fag – watch out for him. I called his mother in for a conference once, and she said he was the only one of her ten kids born with a veil over his head, and that's good luck. Tip number two – do not call parents – they're crazier than their fucking kids."

While the teacher/cop/tax man blabbered on, I fixated on a Thomas Jefferson quote on the wall behind him that said something like education is the antidote to the disease of ignorance. I wondered if the Renaissance man had come into teaching with a pre-existing condition or if he'd gotten infected on the job.

"Call me if you need anything," he said, "I'm the go-to guy around here when Coach and the principal run to Sportsman's to play the ponies."

"I'll count on you," I lied, closing the door. "Hey, by the way, what was your college major?"

"Phys Ed," he said, "I wanted to work for the Park District but teaching paid better."

I returned to reading the cumulative cards of my PZ students – thirty boys and eight girls, between the ages of nine and twelve. I expected to find scribbled notes about Eduardo's allergy to strawberries or Brenda Jean's routine tardiness, but the anecdotal comments, left by previous teachers, noted truancy, multiple school transfers, juvenile detention and incarcerated parents, trifling issues that indicated I just might be in over my head. That flash of insight was replaced by the scarier thought of the imminent influx of my PZ'ers. From the get-go, they needed to know that our classroom was open for business, they needed to think that I knew what I was doing.

I went to the Resource Room to find desks, textbooks, a blackboard and chalk.

"Materials?" asked the assistant principal. "Like what? Like what kind of materials?" He acted as if I'd requested chainsaws.

"Textbooks would be great," I said.

"Scrounge some second and third grade readers – they didn't understand the books the first time around."

"I don't even know where to start scrounging. I'm short thirteen desks."

"Desks you need," he conceded. "The kids have to sit somewhere, but you don't need thirty-eight – absenteeism is high. I'll send a few up later; I'm swamped right now. Downtown sent only half of our book order."

"Please could you maybe send up a blackboard and some chalk?"

"Do you think this is U of C's Lab School? You have the dogs; just make sure they don't get out of the kennel." Noticing my shock, he changed his tone. "Look, I'm snowed under right now, but I think I have some geography books that I could send up when I get a chance. Use them until we get some readers."

Just then the music teacher barged in. "Someone ripped out the keys on my piano. How am I supposed to teach music?"

"Use a flute," the boss responded.

I staggered out of the Resource Room. An ancient busybody, who'd been looking for dictionaries with no success, followed me. "You new teachers kill me. In my day you made do with what you were given. When I didn't have history books, I taught with puppets." She headed to the teachers' lounge for a cigarette.

No readers, or blackboard, a piano without keys, puppets, PZ, spirals – by the end of the day, I figured the conscientious objectors turned teachers would regret burning their draft cards.

The next day school started more or less at nine o'clock though many students adhered to arrive-when-you-feel-like-it. It was not hard to identify the babushka brigade, amazing that Renaissance man got by with only one headscarf. By lunchtime it was obvious that the few students who wanted to learn had come to the wrong place. For the most part, the girls were passive, the boys' speedometers were set between leave me alone and watch out.

Often I wondered why I stayed. I wasn't earmarked for Saigon so I could have hit the door.

Maybe I stayed because I knew these kids could be subjected to much worse. After all, I was literate, drug-free, emotionally stable and I didn't inflict cruel and unusual punishment.

Maybe I stayed because I'd become attached to the kids. I respected eleven-year-olds who fed breakfast to their siblings because mom was sleeping off a bender, students who missed school because they had to baby-sit and wrote their own notes claiming they were absent due to *amonya*. I had a soft spot for eleven-year-olds who read at the first grade level, for kids who were ten going on thirty. I was taken by boys who replaced lost textbooks with stolen library books figuring a book is a book, and besides, who cares? My heart went out to kids who trudged to school on snowy February days wearing gym shoes without socks.

And I adored spunky little girls who trick-or-treated 'til midnight.

I stayed, but for only the year.

The Planet Got A Rave Review

Fueled by the renewed energy of my summer hiatus, I again entered the revolving door of Teacher Personnel. Somewhere in the Windy City, I was certain a school existed where students were not hostages and the principal knew his teachers by name. From a map studded with pins, each of which indicated a teacher vacancy, I spotted a prime location.

The beckoning pin was almost floating on Lake Michigan, just a hop from Chicago's Gold Coast where privileged kids enjoyed advantages that dwarfed their skyscraper abodes. The Magnificent Mile shopping Mecca beckoned from the east, Rush Street, haunt of hipsters, was a mile south and Lincoln Park, a miniature of New York's Central Park, was a stone's throw north.

"Excellent choice," the personnel advisor said, as I handed her the marker of my promising future. "It's an Educational Vocational Guidance Center. Sign this form; assignments are irrevocable. Good luck!"

A week later I reported for duty at the oldest school in Chicago, a weathered landmark which lent a bit of architectural romance to my vision, and reinforced my belief that I stumbled on a gem of a job. The center of the stone stairs was worn by the pounding of thousands of Buster Browns, and the dings and dents in the vintage hardwood floors added to the charm. The main office had old-time, school-house pendant light fixtures suspended over a shiny mahogany counter where employees signed in; a note next to the sign-in sheet announced that there were coffee and rolls in the teachers' lounge and a staff meeting was scheduled at ten.

Over a donut I met my fellow provisional teachers, both men new to the system. The first had graduated Princeton, and looked the part right down to his penny loafers. The other had just completed his doctorate at the Chicago Theological Seminary, and was awaiting ordination.

"The woman in Personnel gave this place a rave review," said the Doctor.

"Yeah, she said it was a great choice," said the Princetonian, dusting powdered sugar off his silk, Ivy-league tie, "but I noticed a lot of vacancies."

A man eavesdropping commented, "I don't suppose one of you brain surgeons thought to ask why there were so many empty slots? Trust me; you won't make it through the year."

"How long have you been here?" asked the minister.

"Fifteen years, but there aren't too many job openings for alcoholics. Don't ever light a match near me." His buddy guffawed. "Like you could pass a breathalyzer," Mr. Doomsday snapped, but he was cut short by the arrival of a man who asked that new teachers come to his office.

"My name is Mr. Sharp. Elijah Sharp. I'm the assistant principal. So what do you want to teach? You're on provisional certificates with no teaching credentials so you can teach anything."

"A college degree with no teacher training qualifies one to teach in all subject areas?" Dr. Divinity asked.

"Yep, pick whatever you want, we need everything. One of you guys want Math? I know women are no good at numbers."

"I'll teach Math," Princeton volunteered.

"Good. Room 204." He turned to Divinity, "You look like a scientist. Room 208. And you, Baby, Language Arts, 301. Now for policy. I'm in charge of discipline. If a kid is causing big trouble, send him down with a note; our intercom is busted. Don't send somebody down for petty nonsense, I'll send him right back."

"What's considered petty nonsense?" Divinity asked.

"Cursing, fighting, threats, pranks, refusing to work – you get paid to be in charge of your classroom."

"What constitutes a serious issue?" asked Princeton.

"Weapons. And only if you see one. If they say something like, 'I'm gonna blow your head off,' ignore it. They talk tough. But if you actually see a knife or gun, send down a note," he said. "And no smoking, but again make sure you actually see the kid with reefer. Sometimes the smell comes from 311 where the street people hang. Keep classroom windows locked. We had a kid who was pushed or fell depending on whose story you buy, from the second story last year. He lived, but he's pretty messed up. Any questions? If not, staff meeting at 10."

An attractive, forty-something woman sat down next to us as we waited for the staff meeting to begin. "Hi, I'm Renee Cross, the librarian," she said. "You must be the new teachers." I didn't know what signaled that we were newbies – Princeton's eye twitch, Divinity's knuckle-cracking or my hair-twirling.

At 10, there were only six of us in the lounge, and two were custodians scarfing down the last of the coffee cake.

The principal entered and launched into a *Welcome to the Family* speech. "Yeah, the Addams Family," a late arrival shouted as he headed to the buffet. "Hey, who ate all the eclairs?"

"Probably fat ass Fred. Pat him down," Doomsday ordered. Two men lifted one of the custodians out of his chair, and began rifling his pants pockets.

"Hey, I found a Long John," yelled a poster child for decaf. "Oops, this isn't a sweet roll, but I'll bet his girlfriend thinks it's one."

The Principal droned on to the finale. "And, in the words of Dr. Seuss, 'Unless someone like you cares a lot, nothing will get better.' Now go get 'em."

Princeton's blinking was now a full-fledged tic. Dr. Divinity's clenched jaw suggested he needed to find a parsonage ASAP.

"Don't let those antics bother you," Renee said. "Some teachers behave worse than the students. We'll go to the Bowl & Roll for lunch, and I'll give you the scoop."

"Nice perk, being surrounded by good restaurants."

"Not exactly surrounded, Cabrini-Green is two blocks thataway," she pointed.

"The housing projects?"

"There's only one Cabrini-Green, the greatest failed social experiment in history, and we get the student casualties from the project's schools – fourteen year-olds reading below third grade," she said. "But things get tricky because Chicago principals get paid by the head; they don't want their numbers to go down so they transfer kids to us only when their behavior is totally off the wall."

Just then the Dr. Seuss enthusiast bellowed from his office, "Move it, folks, I expect appropriate bulletin boards by 3 o'clock!"

"Renee, what's with appropriate?"

"Last year the Shop teachers jig-sawed a life-sized nude and painted WELCOME BACK on a fig leaf."

A woman, with what looked to be an active blonde beehive, was unlocking 304. "Hi," I said, "I'm the new Language Arts teacher."

"I'm the music teacher. Good to have company up here, half the rooms are empty, and no one except the kids and derelicts ever come up to the third floor."

"Derelicts?"

"Addicts, gangbangers – they hang out in 311. The room can't be locked because of the fire escape so all of the dregs in the neighborhood congregate there. Steer clear," she warned. "Can't talk now. I have to see if I got any of the instruments I ordered. There aren't many musical arrangements for kazoos."

"Kazoos?"

"Yes, our trumpets were stolen, the piano has no pedals, the guitar has no strings. Mostly we watch videos – Sound of Music, My Fair Lady."

I decided to check out the 311 halfway house before the squatters commandeered the area.

"You haven't been assigned to 311, have you?" a man, in a Mr. Rogers' cardigan, inquired as I exited the room.

"Oh, no, just checking things out."

"Well, take a peek, then skedaddle. The room gets packed when it's cold out; you can get high just walking down the hall. By the way, I'm Louis Picaro, the art teacher. Everyone calls me Picasso. If you need anything, I'm in room 309."

"As a matter of fact, I do need bulletin board materials."

"Well, someone ripped off my art supplies, but I'll share what's left. Use newspaper for background and it'll be good through Christmas. Staple up paper plates, and tomorrow they'll draw their faces and print their names underneath, that way they get to know each other. In October, have them draw their faces on jack-o-lanterns . . ."

"You're kidding? Pumpkins?"

"Pumpkins, and in November, a giant turkey – they write what they're thankful for on the tail feathers."

The turkey-feather gratitude list was the last straw. I backed away to find Renee.

"I met Picasso *and* Beehive," I said. "Beehive told me about thieves and addicts and kazoos and squatters. Picasso gave me bizarre bulletin board tips."

As we walked to the restaurant, I asked her why she was teaching at the Center.

"Without getting too kumbaya on you, let's just say I believe in giving back."

"I understand trying to make a difference, Renee, but swim in a toxic pool, and you gulp poison."

"Sure, some teachers get warped, but there are good ones too, and a lot of nice kids. Chicken or egg? Politics, incompetence, social conditions, it's all in the water, but we can't just give up."

I liked Renee; she'd been around the block, but she didn't seem jaded.

105

"Okay, I'll try to swim with a snorkel," I said, "but I need the CliffNotes on how this place operates."

By the time we left the Bowl & Roll, I was cycling between concern and curiosity, and running into Mr. Sharp upon our return magnified both.

"Hey, Baby, forgot to mention, no one enters the building before 8:30 – safety issues, and staff vacates at 3:15 sharp! NEVER linger after school."

"But what if a student needs extra help or I have to hold a parent conference?"

He looked at me as though I'd said *but what if I have to convene a NATO Summit?*

"Girl, kick off those red slippers, and buy you some combat boots. You're on a different planet now."

Israel Hernandez Learns to Read

"Israel, I've repeated that word at least six times," I said. "You're making me crazy."

For weeks, I had tried to teach him to read and he'd made no progress.

"Makin' you crazy? How 'bout me? At least you're gettin' paid to do this shit."

"That's true, but I'm not getting paid to bang my head against a wall. Come to think of it, maybe I am."

We both laughed. He was laughing, I'm sure, at the thought of me smashing my head – I laughed because crying was not an option.

Israel was just one of the many students stockpiled in warehouses called Educational Vocational Guidance Centers where I was assigned. If teens hadn't learned to read after a decade in the Chicago school system, and didn't have the courtesy to join the high-school dropout brigade of their own volition, they passed to the Educational Vocational Guidance

Center where they got a lethal dose of shame and boredom and finally pulled the plug on themselves. For some reason, Israel refused to jump ship.

Day after day, this Mexican man-child, his legs bouncing like jack-hammers, sat beside my desk as we slogged through an out-dated pre-primer designed to teach kindergartners. Who cared that black and brown teen-agers had little in common with Dick and Jane though, in this case, the lack of age-appropriate materials didn't explain, but only complicated, Israel's problems.

Long before Attention Deficit Disorder became the go-to diagnosis for kids whose short attention spans and frenetic energy drove teachers crazy, Israel swaggered around the classroom, a roving ambassador of diplomacy, flirting, wisecracking and entertaining those easily amused. As the lone Hispanic in the cadre of black students, he fine-tuned his people skills and charmed even the most hostile competition. He hung out with the "baddest" of the gangbangers, but showed no allegiance to a particular gang, an astounding accomplishment.

Israel threw his lot in with any antisocial scheme which came his way, often cutting classes to head to the near-by Gold Coast to knock hipsters off their $2,000 Colnago bikes. He and Curtiss, his black amigo, would return to class, revved up and sweaty, spouting some cockamamie story about running to Curtiss' crib in the Projects to retrieve a forgotten math book, but the sleek Italian racer, parked in the gym for safe-keeping, announced another mission accomplished.

When cops showed up, Israel was never a suspect because the victim, too shaken to be precise, invariably told the cops he was robbed by a bunch of *black* kids. Since light brown-skinned Israel flew under the radar, he became the hood's Clarence Darrow, launching preemptive strikes to protect his posse.

"These guys didn't do nothin'. Leave 'em alone. We was all in gym class shootin' hoops."

The gym teacher, who never bothered taking roll-call, dittoed the explanation. Flimsy as it was, the alibi worked – the cops avoided reams of paperwork and the flash mob avoided the lock-up. Everybody was happy except for the injured party, but Israel said that the victim should've been happy too, happy that he didn't get killed.

Though he had just begun to sprout peach fuzz, Israel was a seasoned con man. He could sell you the Brooklyn Bridge and demand a tariff for the privilege of jumping off.

"You read good, Miss S, fast, like you got the words memorized," he'd say, "You're the smartest girl I know."

"Thanks, Israel. Now let's finish this chapter."

"I ain't doin' no more today. My brain's tired."

"Your brain would be fine if you'd use it. Let's finish this page."

"I use it, just not in school. Vowels? Come on, ya gotta be kiddin' me. Who gives a fuck?"

"You're right, Israel, this is a stone joke. I have a job to do, and I can't do it without your cooperation. We're wasting our time," I said, closing the book. "I'm done. You don't want to learn to read."

In a flash, his too-beautiful-to-be-wasted-on-a-boy eyelashes fluttered from a breeze of anger, but then, fast as Michael Jordan when he snatched a rebound, he reclaimed his bravado.

"You know, Miss S, you're smart, but you don't know everything. You don't have no clue about not bein' able to read. If you knew, you'd *never* say I don't wanna learn how to read."

"Well, what am I supposed to say? You come in here and clown around, you goof off, you entertain the class with your ridiculous behavior, and I'm supposed to think you care?"

"That's because I don't want nobody to think I care," he stage-whispered, the breeze of anger whirling into a tornado. "I don't want nobody to think I can't learn. Let 'em think I don't give a fuck. But you're smart, Miss S, you should know that's bullshit, you gotta' know not bein' able to read is a bitch."

"I can't even imagine it," I said. "It's got to be a nightmare."

"A nightmare? Nightmare? Really, ya think?" he sneered. "How'd you like to go out on a date and have to say I'll have what-ever she's havin' cause you can't read the menu? Do you have any idea what I do when I wanna' take a girl to the movies and I don't know what's playin' cause I can't read the sign over the Rialto?

'Well, Teach, let me tell you how I do it. I buy a newspaper and I fold it open to the movie part and I go home and I hope that my brother, Hector, is there so I can throw the paper in his lap. 'Find me a good movie,' I say, as I head to the bathroom.

'Find it yourself, asshole.'

'Come on, bro,' I yell from the bathroom. 'I'm in a hurry, I gotta take a shower. Just tell me what's playin'.'

"Hector doesn't know you can't read?" I asked in amazement.

"Nobody knows," he seethed. "Nobody except you. Don't you get it? I'm ashamed. Besides, it's nobody's fuckin' business."

"I had no idea. I'm sorry."

"Sorry? What are you sorry for? It ain't your fault," he said, settling down, as though coughing up his secret had halted the cement mixer in his gut. "You don't have nothin' to be sorry for."

Nothing to be sorry for, I wanted to scream, *you've got to be kidding,* but instead I said, "Israel, I promise we are going to learn to read if it's the last thing we do."

"*We're* going to learn?" he said, flipping back to his cocky persona. "Miss S," he laughed, "you already know how to read. Just teach me, okay?"

"Deal. Tonight I'm going to write a story about this and tomorrow you're going to read it. We'll make a book about you, your stories."

"Cool. We'll call it *Israel and Miss S* – forget *Dick and Jane*. Dick. Can you believe that? Dick. I mean, what kind of fuckin' name is Dick?"

"I'm not going there, Israel. Here's a pass for Social Studies. You're late."

"I ain't goin' to Social. I'm meetin' Curtiss."

"Go to Social. Mr. A. will be mad if you ditch."

"Get real. Mr. A don't even know who's in his class plus he hates me. He says Israel is not a person's name – it's the name of a country. 'From now on, I'll call you Jew,' he said. I told him 'Hey, no problema, man, I'll call you Fuckin' Idiot.'"

Over the next couple of months we turned dozens of conversations into stories. We wrote and read about his family – his brother Hector's new car, his sister Rosita's son, getting busted, his father's accident, Lupe's brutal husband and the first time he read a menu. He wrote a poem about his brother Oscar and a song for his girlfriend. We wrote and he read, stumbling and stuttering, but he *was* reading. "Hey, Miss S," he crowed one day, "do you believe I just read that story about my Ma's cooking, and I didn't fuck up one word?"

There was no stopping him now.

When we finished our **Israel and Miss S** spiral notebook, Israel announced he was going to write his life story. "I'm starting it with the day I was born even though I don't remember that much. I'll get my Ma to help with the details."

Mark Twain said when angry, count to four, when very angry, swear. That Wednesday morning, I was in swear mode. I discovered that some brainiac used a ballpoint pen to draw Gilligan's Island on the long-awaited globe that'd been delivered only two days earlier. I stood there disgusted over the fucked up world I was holding when Curtiss and Leotis charged through the door.

"Miss S, Miss S, Israel shot in the back las' night. He dead."

"Dead? Who? What are you talking about?"

"Israel, Israel Hernandez, he dead. He gone."

"They be washin' his blood right now by the alley on Division Street," Leotis added

I don't remember much more about the day – clusters of kids in the halls, girls crying, boys talking revenge, teachers saying ". . . *what could you expect . . . it was only a matter of time . . ."*

The following day, a note was scotch-taped next to the teachers' sign-in sheet.

ISRAEL HERNANDEZ IS BEING WAKED AT HOME TONIGHT AND TOMORROW. FUNERAL SATURDAY MORNING 10 A.M. ST. DOMINICK'S CHURCH

Mr. A was signing in too.

"Are you going to the wake?" I asked.

"What the hell for?'" He went over to check his mailbox.

Curtiss was in a reflective mood as we walked over to Israel's house after school.

"Where you think he be now, Miss S?"

"Some place good, I hope. Maybe with his father."

"I'm thinkin' he be in heaven. I'm thinkin' God be sayin', 'What the fuck you doin' up here, Lil' Man? Who tol' you you could come here?'"

"Yeah, and he probably told God 'You can't tell me where to go,'" I said remembering his arrogant, defiant side.

"Yeah, I bet Jesus jus' be crackin' up."

The smell of flowers and the food heaped on the kitchen table lent a combination funeral parlor/restaurant air to the space. The hushed quiet of the packed basement apartment was interrupted by sobs as friends joined the crowd. All eyes darted to the entryway, the arrival of a white woman and a black teen-ager stirred whispers. I spotted Hector, an Israel clone right down to the thick eyelashes that had always reminded me of awnings.

"I am so sorry, Hector," I said. "This should never have happened."

For once, Curtiss put his swaggering self on hold as he extended his hand. "Israel be my frien'," he said.

Suddenly, from another room, I heard shrieks of *La maestra! La maestra!* and a little rotund woman, straight out of a Botero painting, shuffled toward me. "La maestra," she kept wailing, as though she was seeing an apparition.

Alternating between sobs and smiles, we spoke through Hector.

"My mother cannot believe a teacher would come to our house," he translated. "She is honored that you come here. She says that Israel told her you were the smartest lady he ever met."

I stood there, unable to cope with the attention and awe, fixated on the drain tile at her feet. "Tell your Mother Israel was a very smart and beautiful boy."

"Si, si," she sobbed. "Muy bonito."

"Tell her he wrote a story about what a good mother she is and he says she's the best cook in the world."

She took my hand and guided me to the wooden coffin which rested on the dining room table and contained the youngest of her children. Standing guard over their baby brother were Lupe, Raul, Juan, Rosita, Oscar, Sergio and Rico. We had written about them all.

Israel lay there, in a sort of mariachi suit – a dark jacket with huge lapels, a narrow string of black leather tied around the collar of a white ruffled-neck shirt, a red satin cummerbund and black pants. Someone had painted a little mustache on his upper lip with eyebrow pencil. His chalky hands held a rosary and his First Communion prayer book. I remembered the story about his First Confession when he'd asked the priest, "So why do I gotta' tell you all this shit?" He was seven years old.

"Let's go, Miss S, come on," I heard Curtiss mumble. "You can't make him come back to school wit' us."

I handed Hector an envelope as we exchanged good-bye handshakes. "You know, Miss S, Israel had stopped throwing newspapers at me," he said, the tears slipping past the awnings.

"Dang, Miss S," Curtiss said as we walked back to school, "Israel be pissed off if he see that Maybelline thing they drawed on his face. He be too cool to look the fool. Why they do that?"

"I guess they wanted him to look like a man – maybe it's easier for them to pretend that he wasn't just a kid."

"Well, he be ashamed if he saw hisself."

"I don't think so, Curtiss," I said, "I know only one thing that Israel was ashamed of, and we were working on that."

Not Good Enough

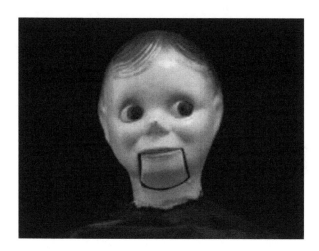

"Who do you think you are? You're not a movie star. This is good enough for you."

A freshman in high school, I was shocked when my dentist bellowed this comment with such fury. I sat in the chair perplexed.

"What are you talking about?" I asked the hulk who was barking in my face. "How do you know what I'm going to be? Why is this good enough for me?" I asked, as I held the small round mirror in my mouth studying the porcelain glob. The blinding, garish light illuminated the tiny white lump that was supposed to pass for a tooth. "This looks okay for a temporary fix, but I don't want this forever."

"If you don't like it, don't come back," he shouted as he yanked the little mirror out of my hand. "No brat is going to come in here and criticize my work!"

Now I was angry. I didn't even care if he told my dad.

"You said you'd fix my tooth," I said as I climbed out of the dental chair. "Don't yell at me because you didn't do it right. This doesn't even look like a tooth – this looks like you painted a tiny piece of Tootsie-Roll white and glued it in my mouth. And don't worry about me coming back," I added, as I ran out the door, "I wouldn't come back if my teeth fell out!"

I cried all the way home – I was going to be in big trouble with my dad who revered the dentist's diploma but my tooth looked like a pencil eraser.

My mother was at the stove. I didn't want to bother her because supper had to be on the table at 4:30 sharp or my father would . . . actually I didn't know what my father would do if dinner wasn't on the table because my mother was never a minute late. No one wanted to irritate a man whose tantrums were legendary. Sometimes his rages were pretty funny – a grown person acting like a spoiled baby – sometimes I'd aggravate him just to see him throw a fit.

"You're home early. Why are you crying," my mom asked as she bustled around the kitchen. "Didn't the dentist give you Novocaine?"

"You won't believe my snaggle-tooth," I sniveled, hardly able to catch my breath. "I'm never going out again as long as I live."

"Oh, stop it – let me see," she said, squeezing my chin and forcing my mouth open. "Well, at least the tooth isn't in the front. You're lucky, you can hardly see it."

"See," I wailed, "even you think it's bad. You can see it when I smile big. I'll have to talk like a ventriloquist."

"Don't be ridiculous. The rest of your teeth are perfect. Are you going to let one little nub botched up by an incompetent upset you?"

I was about to start raving about her calling it a nub, a nub, my own mother calling it a botched-up nub, but I stopped in amazement.

"Did you call Dr. X incompetent?" I asked.

I knew she didn't much care for him. Once I overheard her say to my father, "Jim, the man is so high and mighty. He puts his pants on one leg at a time like everyone else," but she'd never say that in front of us kids.

"Momma, he is incompetent. I told him my tooth looked like a bitsy stub and he yelled that I shouldn't come back, which is fine with me. I hate the guy."

"Watch your mouth," she warned.

"OK, then, I can't stand him. He told me I'm not so important that I need a perfect tooth. He said this tooth is good enough for you."

Hearing that, my mother, who had been hustling to make that 4:30 deadline, spun around from the kitchen sink. I didn't know if the steam came from the pot of scarole she was draining into the colander or from her ears.

"He said what?" she snapped.

"You heard me. He said this ugly tooth is good enough for me."

"Well that bastard," she blurted.

My eyes popped open like one of those push-button umbrellas. My mother never swore. Sometimes she said heck or darn, maybe dammit if she was really ticked, but bastard, never ever. I was shocked, and then, she said it again. "That bastard" – only this time she said it quietly and slowly as though I wasn't even there, as though she was looking at a picture only she could see.

"Quit whining and sit down. We'll get it fixed right," she promised, "but what that bastard said is unacceptable."

Whoa, that was the third time she swore. Was she forgetting that God was listening and she'd be punished? Getting a little nervous – about God, about 4:30 – I said, "Mom, you'd better finish cooking."

"Don't worry about dinner, honey. This is more important," she said, tapping her finger on the kitchen table.

Was she kidding – more important than my dad walking through the door at supper time?

This I had to hear.

"Never let anyone tell you who you are or what you're worth," she seethed. "Never believe anyone who says you're not important – that good enough is good enough for you! That arrogant bastard."

Four times, that was the fourth time! She is playing with fire, I thought, but there was no stopping her.

"That arrogant bastard thinks he can look down on people because he has a couple of capital letters after his name – that he's better than everyone else. He's a poor excuse for a man."

"Mom," I said, "I'm mad, but you're even angrier than I am."

117

Sounds like my Dad with Billy

"That's because I was subjected to bastards like him when I was growing up."

That's it. Here comes the lightning bolt. My father will come in expecting supper and find us slumped over the table.

"I encountered skunks who thought it was okay to treat people like dirt. I had a priest make me stand in the vestibule during Mass because I didn't have a nickel for the collection basket," she said as though she was scooping out a memory she'd buried long ago. "I went to a grocer who switched a loaf of fresh bread for a stale one, and said, 'This is good enough for your mother.'"

Now she was on a tear.

"Years ago, epileptics weren't allowed to go to school. My father died in the 1918 flu epidemic, so my mother had to work. My younger brother suffered seizures. He would come to my school and stare at me through the window. He wanted to be like the other kids, but my teacher said he wasn't good enough to come to school, that I should stay home with him. 'Obviously your grandparents can't handle him,' she said in front of the entire class."

"Mom, stop! They were so mean. I feel like crying."

"I'll stop," she said standing up and kissing the top of my head. "Now set the table," she ordered, noticing the time, "but don't ever forget," she said wagging a finger in my face, "you are better than no one and no one is better than you. That bastard had a hell of a lot of nerve."

Two swear words in one sentence. God must be croaking.

I said a prayer that God would forgive her as I put the last knife and fork on the table and dad walked through the door.

"What smells so good?" he said as he peeked into the pot on the stove and pecked my mother on the cheek.

Turning to hang his jacket, he noticed me sulking at the table. "How was school?"

"School was okay, but look at my ugly tooth," I wailed, stretching my mouth so he could see the mediocre job.

"Give Dr. X time." He yanked down on my jaw to take a good gander. "That's only a temporary, when he's finished it'll look good as new "

"No, Jim," my mother said, "that's the finished product. That jerk's specialty is pulling teeth. He thinks that's all people in this neighborhood deserve. He's a bastard who thinks who he is."

Oh, no, I thought, *jerk, bastard. Dad's going to blow his cork. That's almost worse than getting God angry.*

"Really, daddy, it's true. The tooth is finished," I said trying to stem a tirade, but my dad paid no attention to the swear word. "Dr. X said I'm not a movie star – that this is good enough for me."

"Really?" he said, cocking his head to the side and narrowing his eyes. "Really? He said that? To you? This is good enough for you? Well, after supper we'll pay him a little visit."

I got the feeling my dad was going to go there and have a major tantrum, but I didn't feel one bit sorry for the bully.

He was going to learn that we weren't better than anyone, and no one was better than us. And maybe, Dr. X was just not good enough to be our dentist.

119

You Just Don't Get It

He critiqued women's bodies, shared the math about his own physique and bragged about his sexual exploits ad nauseum. He'd have qualified as the poster child for sexual harassment but for the fact that he was not a child and the term sexual harassment had not yet been coined.

He was my boss; I was sixteen.

He was one of the A&P's star managers, assigned to the Halsted Street store, which was considered a plum because of the store's sales volume. For over twenty years, his bookkeeper had followed him to each new assignment because, as he boasted with a wink, "We have great chemistry." Mary was locked in a miniscule office with this lewd jerk all day, but she was always giggling when we knocked on the door needing singles for our cash registers.

On occasion her giggling would be so loud that they couldn't hear a checker pounding on the door in desperate need of a roll of quarters to make change for an impatient customer. Sometimes we'd have to recruit a bagboy to practically kick down the door, and only then, would Mary's head appear in the little Plexiglas customer service window with her paper A&P chapeau askew. She would fling the coins in our face. "You're not supposed to leave your register without permission."

That snippy attitude was always her undoing because we'd return to our registers and relate the maltreatment to the rest of the crew. When all the teen-aged cashiers were working, we'd even the score by disrupting their afternoon delight. We'd dream up some cockamamie excuses to visit the office, each interruption timed three minutes apart.

First Kitty would knock. "Excuse me, I need a price check." Then Peggy would beat on the door for a check approval followed by Donna interrupting with some piece of junk for the Lost & Found. Finally I'd intrude to turn in a torn bag of candy that I'd found on the magazine rack.

"You kids gonna be in a whole lotta trouble for aggravatin' Mr. Rink," Gert, an older checker, would warn, and, sure enough, the little office door would fly open and, snorting and grunting, the raging bull would stomp into the major arena of the store. His veins would be popping out of his neck, and his eyes would bulge like those little fetal pigs we had to dissect in biology. He would growl out orders giving all the offenders odious tasks.

"Go up and down Halsted Street and bring back our goddamned carts!" he'd yell. "Nobody leaves here tonight until we have every basket accounted for! Disinfect the toilets, scrub down the counters and polish every damn produce scale in this joint no matter how long it takes!"

As Evelyn and the other house pets punched out leaving us to the drudgery, they'd be rolling their eyeballs as if to say, "We told you so. You kids got just what you deserved." But to those of us involved in the caper it was worth every damn minute just to aggravate the crap out of the rotund Romeo and his jowly Juliet.

Life at the A&P though, was not just a series of blue collar Liz Taylor/Richard Burton trysts. It encompassed other oddities that even a naive sixteen-year-old noticed.

At the beginning of the work day, we checkers had to march into the tiny closet-like manager's office, aka the love shack, to store our purses in the safe. No matter how agile we were, it was impossible to escape the lecher's rear-end pats. He must have stayed awake all night planning these pitiful attacks. Amidst squeals and shrieks of *Stop it!* the ladies would scamper to elude his slab-fisted grabs.

His zeal for clamping on for cheap thrills was surpassed only by his penchant for regaling his hostages with the most obscene *jokes*. Not only were his jokes vulgar and offensive, I didn't see how anyone could find them funny. Yet, the women cackled and tittered as if this yellow-toothed buffoon was a Broadway comedian.

Apparently my facial expression did little to hide my feelings of disgust, though the moron chose to interpret my looks of disdain as a lack of appreciation for his comedic flair. Between convulsions of self-induced hysteria over his razor-sharp wit, he would guffaw, "She doesn't get it, she doesn't get it!" and paroxysms of laughter would erupt from the other women.

One day, still seething from his sick comedy shtick, my colleague, Mabel, caught my attention.

"You'd better start laughin' at his jokes, Sweetheart," she said in her southern drawl.

"You're kidding, right?" I asked, thinking she had to be putting me on. She knew how I detested this bully's power trip, which he tried to pass off as "having a little fun with the girls."

"I refuse to encourage his sick routine."

"Just a word to the wise," she said as she bobby-pinned her sailboat-shaped, A&P beanie to her head in preparation for the long work day. "Don't say I didn't warn you." The look on her face signaled she was dead serious.

Mabel was not exactly a barrel of fun. She seldom laughed, except at the boss's jokes. She was a hard, angular woman, genetically emaciated, who lived on cigarettes and Dr. Pepper. Her complexion and hair looked as though they shared the same bar of laundry soap and her hands announced, with their knobby arthritic knuckles, that manicures were out of her league. She would splurge, she said, at the Goodwill Thrift Store on almost-new work shoes because she was on her "hillbilly dogs" all day and, if she didn't take care of her feet, her family wouldn't eat. She always gave more than an honest day's work, never taking an extra minute on a break or punching in a second late and yet, despite earning a decent wage at the A&P, she could never seem to escape the world of bad luck or no luck at all.

Rejected by the hills of Kentucky, her life played like a Hank Williams song, not that Mabel was one to sing the blues. She was, in fact,

123

quite taciturn but sometimes, on our lunch hour in the room where the butchers also gathered to puff on cigars, she would say something that would give me a glimpse of a woman who'd gotten not one single, lousy break in life.

Mabel had graduated from the School of Toughen Up and Too Bad so I was reluctant to ignore her advice about getting with the program, but I was also dumbfounded.

"I can't believe you're telling me to start laughing, Mabel. We should all STOP laughing!" I snipped.

I could tell by the way Mabel dragged on her cigarette that she wasn't happy with my response, but that was too darn bad. With that special brand of righteous indignation unique to those who'd yet to discover that life is not fair, I ratcheted up my protest.

"You should be telling Gert and Evelyn and the other cacklers to knock it off and quit their laughing at these so-called jokes. He's revolting; his jokes are disgusting. They're not funny, Mabel, and I refuse to laugh."

Whereupon one of the toughest women I have ever known shook her Lucky Strike nicotine-stained finger in my face and very slowly said, "Honey, funny ain't got nothin' to do with it. We ain't laughin' 'cause they're funny. I laugh 'cause I have a husband with a bad heart on disability. Angie laughs 'cause her husband had a stroke and a half a him is paralyzed. Gert laughs 'cause she's Colored and good jobs are hard to find." She stubbed out her cigarette in the ashtray, her voice contorted with contempt as she continued. "Evelyn laughs 'cause she's expectin' and her husband walked out on her and her four kids. Mary laughs 'cause she's an old maid and supports her widowed mother and her retarded sister. And you think we ain't gonna laugh at his filthy jokes? You really don't get it, Kid!"

Trapped by Circumstance

"I don't need a University of Wisconsin directory. I need a talented young lady like you to work for me," the man on the other end of the line phone flirted.

Pushing the most recent edition of the UW Alumni Directory, dialing telephone numbers non-stop – busy signals, hang ups, rude refusals – made this alum's response both intriguing and enticing.

The bio of my potential savior noted that he was the owner of a well-known photography studio with an impressive Michigan Avenue address.

"Sir," I responded, "I've had my offer of this directory refused, but I have never had such a creative rejection."

"Rejection? Young lady, you come see me tomorrow and you're hired!" he boomed. I had no idea what his job offer entailed, but escaping the hellhole of tele-marketing was too tempting.

"I will be at your office tomorrow right after work at 5:15," I said.

From sweatshop to Magnificent Mile in one five-minute phone call? This could be the Chicago version of Lana Turner's Hollywood discovery at Schwab's Drug Store. I prayed I was worthy of the opportunity.

The next afternoon I rushed up Michigan Avenue to Valhalla dreaming of working for this prestigious operation. With a bit of luck, I might be able to continue on a part-time basis when I started college in the Fall.

As I ran up the street, I thought of the time I had served at Rockwell Publishing with a hundred quasi-literate dialers, working on commission, elbow to elbow in a boiler room dive hawking this incredibly detailed piece of drek. Even on a good day, it was impossible to make a living wage, never mind my college tuition. Hour after hour we dialed Wisconsin graduates with a canned pitch designed to appeal to memories of their glory days. The spiel was lame, but it was worth listening to if only to hear our preposterous rebuttals when an alum was reluctant to waste his money.

If, for instance, someone said he couldn't afford the directory because his house burned down, and he was destitute plus he just found out his wife was the arsonist who wanted him incinerated to collect on his insurance so she could run off with his best friend, I would have a perfect response. Even if he added he was contemplating suicide.

"Sir, now more than ever you need this directory. You cannot pass on this incredible resource. It is filled with names of contractors who will rebuild your torched house, stockbrokers who will make you wealthy, financial planners, divorce lawyers, criminal attorneys who will put your ex-wife in jail, insurance agents who will write a policy that will make your spouse wish she'd not acted so precipitously, and psychiatrists who will help you deal with the pain of betrayal by your best friend. And the support team will all be Badgers eager to assist a Badger brother."

If, by then, the alum wasn't begging for a copy of the directory, I'd continue.

"You will also have this handy referral to help you when you begin dating – hundreds of educated women who need not make money in the sleazy way your soon to be ex-wife tried, women who will renew your will to live – cultured women who share your love for your alma mater bonding with you during Wisconsin football games.

I guarantee you will regret not having purchased the leather-bound edition since your copy will be dog-eared from constant use reaching out to your Badger family who share your Badger pride!"

Fortunately most of the alumni didn't have such complicated problems, but I did use some variation of the above on most solicitations. Sterling Catch, who offered me the job, hadn't even heard my dazzling sales pitch. What impressed him so that he wanted to hire me sight unseen? Was it my precise diction? My sophisticated delivery? Did he detect the conviction in my voice?

But it didn't matter. Right then, as I hurried along Boul Mich, my focus was on my lucky break.

The address reeked of status and respectability. After a cursory interview, Mr. Catch told me that I'd start the next day. Having asked nothing about my education and/or experience, I figured he was just an excellent judge of raw talent though he was a bit vague about my job responsibilities.

"Familiarize yourself with the studio while I work out the details. I"m designing a job just for you."

A job. created. specifically. for me? I was awestruck.

Until I realized that Mr. Catch was kind of an anti-Statue of Liberty, who welcomed the hungry and tired, as well as the naive and stupid.

Apparently years before, he had been the photographer of choice for the North Shore's upper crust, but his top of the heap days were behind him. After succumbing to too many glasses of bubbly and a plethora of sweet, young things, he was left only with arrogance and extraordinary sales skills. If Mother Teresa herself appeared in his studio, he would have tried to seduce her and, if rebuffed, he would immediately shift into Super Salesman mode and offer her, at a greatly reduced price because of the sheer volume, individual portrait sittings of every forlorn wretch who had ever crossed her path.

Something in his life had gone awry resulting in vanities and character defects so enormous that even an Oprah intervention would have been wasted. He targeted the pathetic and his staff perfectly reflected his predatory proclivity.

Mandi was the Anna Nicole look-alike receptionist who had been married and divorced so many times she stopped changing her last name because of all the paperwork. She was late a lot and had many court dates. Her complex child-support and alimony arrangements, she said, required frequent tweaking, but I suspected the chronic tardiness and incessant lawyers' calls had more to do with her nighttime activities.

Mort, the genius retoucher, smoked in the darkroom, and, I reckoned, drank the photo-developing chemicals in there as well. Like a mole, he ventured out of the darkness only occasionally, blurry-eyed and shaky, searching for ". . . that bastard Sterling!" who routinely demanded he do the impossible.

A munchkin widow who would disappear for days, Theodosia Goodsell, was afflicted with self-diagnosed *neuralgia*, soothed only by fifths of gin. When she showed up in working condition, her sales skills put even Mr. Catch's to shame. She would call on the recently bereaved and offer them a once in a lifetime opportunity to order an outrageously overpriced oil painting of their newly deceased loved one. Her frequent slugs from her thermos of *cough syrup* while telephoning potential patsies led to more than a few bizarre appointments.

Irene, the resident artist, who executed these paintings was responsible for making the bereaved's dream a reality. She spoke five languages fluently, but only enough English to keep us confused. Her salad days were spent fleeing the Nazis and now, because she'd lost everything in the war, including her academic credentials, she was reduced to painting over huge enlargements of snapshots. Often the head of the subject in the original photo was pea-size and Mr. Catch would insist Mort blow it up to 16x20, which obliterated the facial features. It was Irene's job to paint a face that would be somewhat recognizable to the widow. Much of the time, not because of Irene's lack of expertise, the finished portrait would make a paint-by-number picture look like an Art Institute masterpiece.

Completing the off the wall cast was Evelyn Bates, a society woman who'd fallen on hard times. She never quite came to grips with the fact that misfortune had relegated her to soliciting portrait sales from survivors of the dead. She took great pains to maintain the pretense of working "just to keep busy . . ." but her hopelessly outdated wardrobe, and tales of forty-years past soirees signaled her denial.

It was an unusual group, but even more peculiar was the fact that there was no photographer on staff. Instead we had a series of photographers who would apply for the "vacancy," work like demons during their unpaid month-long "audition" photographing weddings, bar mitzvahs and debutante debuts and pray they'd get hired. They would cover a variety of events so Mr. Catch could get a "valid sample of your work," but, alas, at the end of a month they never quite had what it took. "You are a competent photographer, but you're missing that *certain something*," Mr. Catch would say. "You're just not a good fit for my North Shore clientele." It was a brilliant never-fail scam.

So there we worked, the *Cabinet of Dr. Caligari,* a talented addict, a wacko single mother, an ancient alcoholic widow, a delusional has-been with a dying husband, a displaced person who'd lost everything in the war, an "auditioning" photographer and a broke college kid.

Trapped by circumstance, desperate for work, we were a captive crew ripe for exploitation which Mr. Catch scented like a foxhound.

Outside of the events captured by the *probationary* photographers, the dearly departed were the headliners. In the days when Kodak Brownie box cameras were considered high tech, when certain socio-economic groups cherished a snapshot of a loved one the way blue-bloods revered a John Singer Sargent portrait, Mr. Catch carved a predatory niche long before Bernie Madoff picked pockets.

Out of Respect

I've had my share of culture shock as I traipsed through Europe, the Americas and the Middle East but nothing could have prepared me for my first encounter with a burqua clad woman on a flight from Rome to Beirut. Not pictures, not books, not stories – nothing could have prepared me for the searing image of the ghostly apparition.

A fastidiously groomed man in a Savile Row suit, Gucci loafers and a Rolex guided the ethereal shroud to its seat. Swathed head to ankle in a voluminous black cover replete with a plastic Darth Vader-like screen masking its face, it seemed like a character in "Night of the Living Dead."

When the meal was served, her gloved hands flipped part of her veil forward creating a mini-tent under which she ate. Except for her feet, you would never have known it was a person – no skin, no arms nor legs, no voice.

I was simultaneously fascinated and repulsed though I'm not sure which part of the scene prompted my visceral reaction. After all, growing up with nuns exposed me to some very unusual attire and I was steeped in a religion which routinely vilified women as "occasions of sin" so it wasn't as though misogyny was exactly foreign to me.

Maybe it was the proud, pristine peacock steering the faceless, formless figure down the aisle. Maybe it was the innocent faces of their children who would soon learn that, at puberty, the boys would become men and the girls would disappear. Maybe it was the realization that a change in geography could make any woman, myself included, an erasable nonentity. Maybe it was the neon jelly slippers that peeked from beneath the capacious black robe. Whatever it was, it overwhelmed my heart.

In Beirut, I shared the encounter with my Egyptian friend, Mohsen. "Ah," he explained, "we Arabs respect virtuous women – that is why we require the burqua."

Oh. My. God.

Years later, my daughter told me about helping to plan a *Take Back the Night* rally on campus.

"Hundreds of students," she explained, "will protest violence against women. We're going to chant 'Yes means yes! No means no! However we dress, Wherever we go!' It's about victimization," she declared, "about empowerment, too. But really, Mom, I think it's about respect, don't you?"

"Yes, Lia, it is about respect," I replied, flashing back to the image tattooed on my soul so long ago. "Americans don't always get it right, but we do keep trying."

Don't compromise yourself.
You are all you've got.

— *Janis Joplin*

Confessions of a Serial Forwarder

I am done. Finished. Fini.

I will never pass on another funny joke, lifesaving tip, critical warning or virus threat. Call me selfish, but I'll not even pass on a Code Red Alarm. I will no longer be the Paul Revere of the Internet. I will not attempt to brighten anyone's day nor feel compelled to tell acquaintances that, like a thousand helium balloons, their friendship lifts my heart. I will not pass along Amber Alerts or Novenas to St. Dymphna, patron saint of psychotics.

I was never an irresponsible forwarder. I regularly snopesed things that came my way. If I got an email that claimed women who'd had breast augmentation survived the Titanic because their breasts served as life jackets, I verified it before hitting the **SEND** button.

I didn't fall for the promises of a cash windfall if I prayed for our soldiers in Iraq. I didn't believe I would contract leprosy if I let the flame on the Candle for World Peace, which has been circulating on the net since October 8, 1937, burn out. I didn't betray confidences about my friends' husbands who were undergoing sex-change surgeries or blabber about my manager's son who was working his way through mortuary school by selling crystal meth.

I only disseminated material that would cheer-up shut-ins, brighten the days of the depressed and/or enlighten my colleagues. And I never shot-gunned messages to my 174 best friend contact list. I meticulously tailored my forwards to special interest groups – recipes to the Julia Child devotees, Amber Alerts to those who cared about their children, warnings to pet lovers about tainted cat food from China.

In short, I was cyber responsible which is why this slip has shattered me.

My friend, an ex-nun, forwarded a story about two old ladies in a nursing home. It was not in the best of taste so I was extra careful. I judiciously selected several girlfriends who enable my forwarding addiction, and clicked *bcc.* I refused to be known as the wreckless forwarder, one whose name on the *You've Got Mail* screen prompts **DELETE**. I abhorred indiscriminate forwarders who willy-nilly sent pictures of nursing baby cows whether or not the recipient was into bovines.

I was prolific, but selective except for this one freaking time I goofed up.

My, oh my, you do have quite a sense of humor the message said.

Please. God. No! I thought as I stared in horror at the computer screen. In a flash, I realized that, in my forwarding frenzy I inadvertently bcc'ed the name directly above my friend Susan's, a minister/psychotherapist professional acquaintance.

"George," I shouted as I ran up to our bedroom, "you are not going to believe this – I am mortified. Wake-up! I want to die!"

He continued to snore.

"George," I shrieked, flipping on the light switch and tearing off his blanket, "wake up! I am totally humiliated. I can never show my face again! Get up – this is a disaster."

"Lower your voice and turn off the damn light," he growled, not at all grasping the gravity of the situation. "It's midnight. What the hell is wrong with you?"

"I just got an email from Rev. Grier, Dr. Grier," I cried, kneeling at the side of our bed. "I cannot believe I did this. I am so stupid! I should not be allowed to own a computer. I am an idiot!"

"Could you please save the self-flagellation for the morning? I have to be up at six."

"Oh, you don't care! You don't care that I've just humiliated myself – that I may have to live in a cloister for the rest of my life. Please! Sit up at least," I said, turning the ceiling fan on high to get his attention.

Suddenly it was as though we were in front of a jumbo jet on the tarmac at O'Hare. Olivia, my cat, had come in to investigate the ruckus only to have her long hair blown back as though she were in a wind tunnel.

It worked.

He got up and stomped over to the fan switch almost twisting the knob off the wall. "Okay, okay. I'm awake. I do care. I'm very interested in why you're suicidal."

"I accidentally forwarded a really, really offensive email to Dr. Grier. I mean really offensive! I'm so embarrassed I could die!"

"I warned you about sending that shit out all the time. Why do you insist on forwarding that crap?"

"I can't help that I'm easily amused and besides, it's not crap – they're little jokes that just might bring a bit of sunshine into people's lives."

"Sunshine? If your friends need your junk mail to bring a smile to their faces, they're in bigger trouble than you. Why don't you just stick to sending out computer viruses?"

"Thanks a lot. I'm glad you woke up to tear me down," I said in my best Meryl Streep voice. "I told you it was an accident. Do you think I wanted to send him an email about two old ladies in a nursing home?"

"Old ladies in a nursing home? Are you nuts? Look, I'm sorry if you think I'm tearing you down, but you are a maniac on that computer. It's a wonder you have any friends left who will even open your stuff."

"Well," I said haughtily, "I happen to have 174 friends in my address book. I'll bet you don't have half that."

"Look, I'm not having this stupid-ass conversation at this hour. Let's get some sleep."

"Sleep? No, no, listen to me! You haven't heard the joke. It's so outrageous I wish I could go into witness protection," I moaned. "Okay, just listen and tell me it's not so bad."

"You don't get it! I NEED SLEEP. I don't care about this nonsense! I do not care about your joke. I have a life!"

His insensitivity never ceased to amaze me.

"Please, I'm begging you. Just listen. Two old ladies in wheelchairs were in a nursing home. One old lady asks the other, *'Do you ever get horny?'* The other says, 'Yes.' So the first old lady says, *'What do you do about it?'* and the second old lady says, *'I suck on a Lifesaver.'* and the first old lady says, *'Who drives you to the beach?'"*

For a minute there was dead silence. He stared at me as though I were a postal worker with a gun. I could tell he was counting to a hundred. Finally he said quietly, "Well, wasn't this a car crash waiting to happen."

And that's why I will never again forward anything as long as I live. I don't care if someone sends me a YouTube of Barbara Bush giving Barack a lap dance, I swear I will not pass it on.

Okay, maybe I'll forward the URL, but believe me, that's it.

Miracle in a Bottle

"Come on, sit down – free demonstration – **Botox in a Bottle** – take ten years off your face," the blonde in cowboy boots, a zebra-striped smock and foot-long hair extensions shouted to the women jamming the aisles at the Jewelry Show. "This product is guaranteed to give a knock-out punch to Mother Nature. Use this amazing, all natural Botox magic and your husband won't recognize you."

Despite my looking out of the corner of my eye, pretending not to pay attention to her rap as I walked by the booth, she scented, like a rat-terrier, a live one. She grabbed my arm with her dagger-like fingernails and pulled me over. "Honey," she boomed over her lapel microphone, "you look like you have some extra mileage. I can banish it in seconds. Sit down, I'll erase twenty years."

The thought of looking like my daughter's sister was seductive. I bit.

"Twenty years?" I joked as a I obeyed. "I'll look like I'm nineteen."

"Dream on, Babe. Look up at the ceiling," she commanded, as she continued her sales pitch in a hybrid Brooklyn/British accent. "I'm applying the **Botox in a Bottle** around the eye area, ladies, where this poor woman has bags, lines and crow's feet. Stick around five minutes and you'll witness a miracle."

This androgynous vampire had a Ph.D in destroying confidence – in a flash I was ready to beg *Please, please salvage the wreckage.* With the pads of her fingertips she tap, tap, tapped the life-saving serum around my eye area while she blathered on without taking a breath. "Take a chair, Ladies. **Botox in a Bottle.** Apply it all over your face – change your life. Firms sagging skin, lifts jowls, eliminates laugh lines – gives you a glow like you haven't seen since you first had sex." As she continued to tap, tap, tap, she cautioned, "Tap the golden serum lightly, Girls, you don't want to make your skin any worse than it is."

I sat there blinded by the ceiling's klieg lights wondering why I was participating in this fiasco with a trout-lipped woman who looked like a drag queen.

"You're almost finished, Doll. The **Botox in a Bottle** just has to dry," she said manically flapping a piece of cardboard over my left eye to speed the process. "There you go, Sweetheart, all done," she chortled thrusting a miniscule mirror into my hand. "Look at that eye, Ladies," she screeched at the crowd as they pushed and shoved to get a closer look at the magical transformation. "Grab a chair, and I'll take ten years off you too."

Ten years? She promised me twenty, I thought as I stared into the mirror, my mind imagining worst-case scenarios. *Maybe I had more miles than I thought, maybe I needed a more serious intervention . . .*

"Your eye looks fabulous," she gushed, just as I was thinking I might need to wear a burqua until I could track down a plastic surgeon. "This product works miracles – the difference between night and day!"

I had to admit the Botoxed eye looked different, though I couldn't decide exactly how. Before I had a chance to study it, she pulled the mirror out of my hand.

"I knew you'd love it," she shrieked. "I've got a Show Special here for $100 – you get two ounces of **Botox in a Bottle** – a month's supply. You'd pay twice that at Neiman's for half as much."

I could feel the skin under my eye tightening, sort of shriveling. I thought of Miss Havisham in *Great Expectations.*

The pitbull in rose-colored, aviator glasses sensed my hesitation. "Because your face needs quite a bit of help, I'm going to throw in a bottle of **Power Peptides.** Tired, sick, too many Cosmotini's last night? This will deflate those bags and inflate your mood in seconds."

The beauty maven was on a roll now. "And because you seem like a lady who loves a bargain, I'll give you absolutely free, a bottle of **Synergistic Serum** which will erase age spots, smooth mottled skin and leave your complexion baby soft – kind of like taking a wire brush to your face without the pain. You get the entire kit for $100 if you buy right now. This is a once in a lifetime opportunity. How many kits would you like?"

"Well, I am impressed with your product," I stammered, which was somewhat true because I could kind of feel my eyelid lifting, "but I want to see what my friend thinks."

"My name's Destiny, Botox – booth 410. You'll be back, Sweetie," she predicted, as I split to hunt down Susan.

Twice a year, Susan and I attacked the Jewelry & Apparel Show with military precision. Familiar with the layout and the vendors, we had our routine down pat: valet park, flash show badges, agree to meet up in two hours at the food court, keep cell phones handy in case we needed a second opinion on a purchase before our agreed upon rendezvous.

Hurry c my eye – 410, I texted.

Two minutes later, I spotted Sue hustling down Aisle 400. "This had better be good," she warned. She didn't like being bothered when she was power shopping.

"I want your opinion." I turned toward some near-by halogens and whipped off my sunglasses.

"What the hell happened? Your eye looks swollen. Are you getting a sty?"

"Sty? Look at my crow's feet."

"You don't have crow's feet."

"That's because I just had a **Botox in a Bottle** treatment," I stage-whispered.

"No, Mar, you've never had crow's feet," she insisted.

"The Bottle Botox Lady studied them under her Skinscope. She said they're developing rapidly," I whined.

"Don't tell me you let that RuPaul look-alike near your face. Why would you waste five minutes in her chair when you could have been shopping?"

"She said this **Botox in a Bottle** could dramatically reduce my laugh lines, frown lines and lip lines on contact."

"Did she tell you you'd look like a cyclops?" Susan scoffed.

"You don't understand hope in a bottle – I don't know why I ask for your opinion. You're not that into beauty breakthroughs."

"Well I am into rip-offs and this Botox miracle qualifies. You broke my shopping momentum; I'm done for the day. Are you finished yet?"

"Yes, I just want to stop on the way out to pick-up the Show Special," I declared still clinging to the vision.

"Oh, let me guess. A one-time Show Special and, if you purchase right now, she'll throw in two bottles of some other crap."

"Did you see the demo too?" I smirked, thinking I wasn't the only one lured by the promise of eternal beauty.

"No, I watch infomercials. Ever heard of the one hour Lifestyle Lift?

"Susan, this is not some kind of Sham-Wow hype. This is based on scientific anti-aging research. A chemist discovered these products."

"Chemist? You must be kidding. Who's the chemist – oh, never mind – I bet it's Amy Winehouse."

"You're no help. Let's go. If George and Lia are impressed with my eye when I get home, I'm coming back tomorrow."

"Fine," she said, steering me toward the exit.

On the ride home I caught a glimpse of my eye in the car's side mirror. It looked a bit unusual, but it was a cloudy day.

My husband and daughter would be able to see the transformation. I hoped Destiny would honor the "if you buy right now" special and wouldn't tell me she was sold-out the next day.

I found my daughter at her computer. "Lia, I'm going to take off my sunglasses. I want you to look at my eyes, and tell me if you notice anything."

"Mom," she exclaimed, "DO NOT BORROW MY MASCARA! You have pink eye!"

"I don't have pink eye. Look UNDER my eye."

"What am I looking for? Bags?"

"Never mind," I snapped as I went off to find her father. I should have known better than to think a twenty-something would understand an aging prom queen's terror of gravity, much less understand our "men ripen; women rot" culture.

George was in the den reading.

"Hi," he said as he glanced up. "Have fun at the Jewelry Show?"

So much for the pitbull's claim that "your husband won't even recognize you." He knew exactly who I was.

"George, put the Kindle down, and tell me what's different about me."

Without looking up, he said, "You bought a new necklace."

"No," I said. "Please put down the book and take a good look at my face."

"You got your hair cut?"

"Wrong. Do not look at my head. Look at my face," I said in a You've Got Mail voice. "What do you notice?"

Realizing I was not going away, he looked up and stared. "Your left eye looks beady – it's smaller than the other one. Put an ice-pack on it."

My family was hopeless. What made me think they'd comprehend the heartbreak of watching the bloom fade, especially when one didn't have a lot of bloom in the first place. The mirror in the den did make my eye look a little weird, but overhead lighting is never flattering.

I went to my room, despair dampening my dream, when I noticed my furry friend curled up on my bed grooming her privates. On more than one occasion, I had confided my insecurities, my problems, and she'd always told me the truth.

"Olivia, I need your opinion. I want to buy *Botox in a Bottle*, but I'm not sure it works." She stopped licking. Her peridot peepers opened wide. Her purr confirmed she knew this was important.

"What do you think of my left eye?"

"Normally I don't judge," she hissed, "but, I swear on a salmon, you look peculiar. Go to the bathroom and take a gander."

She jumped onto the vanity to assess the situation. In the brightly illuminated medicine chest mirror, I finally accepted the truth. My under-eye looked like a shattered windshield. The serum had solidified into a fractured varnish-like finish. Destiny had told me the product would stay on until I took it off, but she failed to mention that, by the end of the day, I'd look like Dorian Gray.

"You know," Olivia meowed, "Emerson said that the sweetest music is played on the oldest fiddles."

"Sometimes you can be so hateful," I cried. "You could at least show a bit of sympathy. Is it a sin to not want to look like a freaking hag – to stay a step ahead of Father Time?"

"It's not a sin – it's an impossibility. You're going to have to accept yourself as you are. Look at me," she purred, "I am perfect. I'm one of a kind. There's not another animal on the planet that compares to me," she declared, swishing her tail, "and you are perfect, too."

"That's easy for a Persian to say – you don't have to worry about jowls, dull skin, drooping eyelids . . ."

"Oh, stop it!" she hissed. "I'll give you a tip. Mix a little litter with water – it's like putty – fills craters, skim-coats wrinkles. That's how Cher keeps her face together; Michael Jackson used it too."

And then she added, very cattily, "Never mind, just buy the crap. It sure can't hurt."

Bionic-Footed Mom

The logic behind an obese woman torturing herself in a girdle to look five pounds thinner always escaped me, but my reasoning skills vanished when it came to shoes. At 5'1" I counted on platforms to give me that long, lean look.

As newlyweds, we traipsed through Central and South America with me teetering on platform espadrilles or prancing on high-heeled sandals. Looking good was ever so important when crawling through ruins, and crawl I did. Had it not been for an eighty-three year old Yale professor lending me a hand as we trudged to Machu Picchu, I'd have been limping on my own.

After delivering his umpteenth "I do not understand your insistence on wearing those freaking shoes . . ." lecture, my 6'2" sanctimonious and sensibly shod spouse time and again left me in the dust. His admonitions only stopped when he became weak from altitude sickness (a big problem for tall people) and I transformed into the little pack mule lugging our bags through Peru and Colombia.

By the time we returned to the States I was ready for orthopedic boots, but I was a slow learner. I continued sashaying in bound-feet type shoes for many more years until foot surgery and titanium rods brought my platform fetish to a halt.

I was delighted when my daughter sprouted past me as an adolescent. When she carried flip-flops to her prom "just in case," I knew I had raised a practical fashionista capable of standing on her own two feet.

Sometimes We Jump

"This is not a good idea," I said to my daughter, certain my advice would be ignored.

Her illegal alien friend was handing over one of his many part-time jobs he no longer wanted. That she thought being the delivery girl for Toppi Thai Restaurant was the perfect job for a college student amazed me, despite the fact that I had witnessed many of her imprudent decisions in the past.

"Mom," she tried to convince me, "Pablo says I can make $50 to $120 a night for 4 hours work. No taxes. I can study between deliveries. You are being a snob. This is a very cool job."

"Cool job? Are you kidding? Lia, think about the wear and tear on your car, the teen-agers who will tip you a quarter, driving in bad weather, the horrendous cost of gas, creepy strangers coming to the door . . ."

"Mom, you're being negative. I'm taking the job."

Not a month into this lucky break, Lia became disenchanted with rude customers, poor tippers, mean dogs, wrong addresses, and kitchen help hitting on her. Just another day in Paradise I thought.

I ignored her complaints, though one day her grievance did send me into high gear.

"Mom," she wailed into the phone, "you won't believe this!"

"Were you robbed? Did you have an accident?" I shrieked, projecting my worst fears. "Are you okay?"

"I'm fine, but you won't believe what just happened. I walked into Dr. Cannon's office to make a delivery and the receptionist looked at me and started screaming, 'We didn't order Mexican food! We don't want Mexican food!' She went crazy."

"Why did she say that?" I asked bewildered.

"I guess she took one look at my Colombian skin and assumed I was delivering Mexican food."

"You have got to be kidding," I gasped, offended not only for myself but for her, my adopted daughter, as well. "That's incredible!"

"I know, Mom, I was shocked too. The lady went ballistic."

"Lia, what did you do?"

"I just told her to calm down – that I was delivering their Thai food."

"That's all you said?"

"What could I say, Mom? The lady was just stupid."

"Lia, I would have thrown the food on the floor; I would have turned around and walked out," I said, jumping into my self-righteous, anti-discrimination mode. "She saw brown skin and assumed you were delivering Mexican food? Tomorrow I'm calling Dr. Cannon's office to let her know she has a racist moron sitting at the front desk. The woman should be fired," I ranted.

"Mom, stop. I told her it was Thai food and she settled down."

"Lia, I would have opened the container and dumped it on her desk."

"Mom, that's crazy. Why would I behave like that?"

"Lia, to assume someone is delivering a certain kind of food based on the color of her skin is outrageous. What would she say to a Black person who was delivering egg foo yong? What would she say to an Oriental pizza driver?"

"Mom, if she has something against brown skin, that's her problem. Who cares if she's prejudiced? I just won't deliver there anymore. You're overreacting."

"I am not overreacting. I just hate jerks."

"Then you're prejudiced, Mother, prejudiced against jerks. If I'd known this was going to upset you, I wouldn't have told you. I only shared it because I was so taken aback. The lady is pathetic."

"Pathetic? Your illegal friend probably passed the job on because he'd met one too many Neanderthals."

"No, Mom. Pablo gave me the job because his driver's license expired and he couldn't afford to get another counterfeit one. Did you know counterfeit documents cost a fortune?"

"Lia, I can't even believe we're having this conversation. You're making me crazy. Would you please quit this stupid job?" I begged, smoke coming from my ears. "We'll talk later, I have to go."

I slammed down the phone, desperate to share my fury.

"Why don't you find something else to worry about?" my husband suggested when I related the egregious offense. "Lighten up – it's not illegal to be an insensitive clod," he said blowing off my tirade.

"Lighten up, *lighten up*? You're telling me to *lighten up* when some ignorant wretch slaps our daughter in the face because of the color of her skin? You have the audacity to tell me to lighten up?"

"Calm down. You are overreacting."

"Overreacting? So you think I'm overreacting? You reduce my outrage to overreacting? I could just scream!"

"You are screaming, Honey. Don't get so excited. Did it ever occur to you that the woman might be allergic to tacos or maybe was having a bad day?"

"Oh, a bad day, that's a good one – a bad day justifies racism," I seethed. "Maybe if more people took action when they witnessed something like this, maybe if more people stood up . . ."

He cut me off. "Oh, I get it. This is your new action plan – dumping food on the floor. Flinging a piece of moo satay in someone's face is fighting injustice. That is absolutely brilliant!" he declared, eyeing me as though I were some kind of unbalanced bag lady. "Saul Alinsky must be rolling over in his grave," he said referring to a legendary iconoclast.

"Okay, make fun of me. You know I'm not advocating throwing pad thai in people's faces although, come to think of it, that'd be a novel way

149

of dealing with disparate treatment," I said just to push my husband a little closer to the edge where I was already standing. "Oh, no, now I get it. You're mocking me because you envy my pluck."

"Pluck? Don't you think it a bit strange to make some tactless person's aversion to Mexican food into a hate crime?"

Just then the phone rang.

"Mom, you're not going to believe this."

"Please, Lia, I can't take any more tonight – I'm too aggravated."

"Listen, Mom, just stop and listen. This is the best. You know that Toppi owns Toppi Thai, right? And that her husband owns La Lupita?"

"Yes, I know that, Lia, we've eaten there many times."

"Well, not anymore. La Lupita went out of business last week and Toppi is using La Lupita's leftover bags. When I delivered to Dr. Cannon's office I was carrying a La Lupita bag with a logo that says 'THE BEST MEXICAN FOOD IN TOWN.' The lady wasn't commenting on my skin – she saw the bag," she laughed.

"Oh-my-god, Lia. That is unbelievable. Imagine if I'd called Dr. Cannon. She'd have thought I was a lunatic demanding the receptionist's head on a plate."

"Imagine if I'd dumped the food on the floor, Mom, that would have been so awful. I can't believe you gave me such bad advice." Then, going for the jugular, she proceeded, "I think you let your emotions get in the way. You tell me to count to ten before I act, but you need to count to a thousand," she lectured. "You're too quick-tempered. You're not just a reactor, you're a nuclear reactor."

I had it coming. "I apologize, Lia."

"No problem, momma bear, just remember I don't look like Goldilocks."

Don't Be Cruel

"Ma'am," the lady from the Visitors Center responded, "This is Elvis Week. There ain't a room for miles around – not even one with a bathtub never mind a swimmin' pool. Why the whole town is jam-packed. Fans come from all over the world!"

Welcome to Graceland, a place we'd managed to avoid but finally agreed to visit thanks to the relentless badgering of Gianna, our 12 year-old Elvis groupie. Because Elvis had been dead for decades, I assumed he had few fans left so I made no hotel reservations.

We had four little girls in tow, our daughters, Gianna and Lia and their friends Amy and Elise. It had stormed the last 400 miles; *no room at the inn* was the last thing I needed to hear. My husband's twitching eyes suggested he was a bit on edge, and the *are we there yet* and *we're hungry* whines were not helping matters. The single stroke of luck was that I'd walked into the Visitors' Center alone and no one else heard the dire news. If my husband found out that I'd not booked a hotel during Elvis Week, he'd go ballistic. I prayed for an on-the-spot miracle as I climbed back into the van.

A drenched purple dinosaur was waving people into the Family Fun Buffet parking lot. "There's Barney!" I cheered, "Let's eat here!" With the sigh of a martyr, George turned into the parking lot.

"Go ahead and get a table while I stop in the Ladies Room," I yelled as they tore out of the van and streaked through the monsoon. As I hopped out, I slipped and plopped into a puddle. The soggy dinosaur waddled over to help. "M'am, let me give you a hand – you look like you're in trouble." *Oh Barney, if only knew.*

Limping into the restaurant, I found the Yellow Pages and started dialing. I hit pay dirt on the seventh hotel. Yes, they had a room and they were located right across from Graceland! Across from Graceland – a miracle in motion.

I found George cradling his head in a booth. Each of the girls was inhaling a plate of desserts – cupcakes, pie, brownies, ice cream, Jell-O and cookies – all smothered in marshmallow fluff.

I winced at George's willingness to let the inmates run the asylum, but I didn't want to push my luck with a lecture on nutrition. Instead I herded everyone back to the van and gave George directions to the Graceland Hotel.

"How did you find this place?" my husband asked as we turned into the parking lot. Huge, burly men in uniform surrounded the property. "It looks like they have good security," I observed.

"Good security? Are you nuts? They're carrying shot-guns."

"Maybe the hotel wants to discourage fans from running across the highway to use the bathrooms."

Later I learned of Graceland's unusual historic odyssey. When a local doctor built what was to become Graceland, the property was in a rural area far outside Memphis. Years later when Elvis bought the house, Memphis had grown some, but the area was still a good distance from town and semi-rural. In the last three decades, however, Memphis had grown by leaps and bounds and Graceland now sat in the middle of a rough, drug-riddled section of the city.

We walked past the armed militia to the front desk.

"You have a reservation for Edwards," I said, gawking at the desk clerk's inch long pinkie nails.

"Yeah. Room for six. $600."

"$600? You must be joking," I blurted. "I mean, if it's not too much trouble, may we see the room?" I did not need to get on the wrong side of this guy.

"Okay," he shrugged, "we'll take the stairs – elevator ain't workin'."

"This place gives me the creeps," George muttered as we made our way up the dingy stairwell. "It's either a drug den or a whorehouse."

"It's convenient to Graceland," I whispered, "we'll push a dresser in front of the door."

We exited the stairwell, creeping along like a company of moles. The hall smelled of cigars and sweat. The carpeting was threadbare and stained.

When the intimidating desk clerk unlocked the room, the kids tore past us and immediately stripped to their swimsuits. I wanted to accept this room, but a layer of grime covered the bedspread, carpeting and windows.

I had to think of a diplomatic way to back out of this deal without aggravating the frightening thug.

"Girls," I called to the boisterous brood, "we can't stay here. We need more beds," I added, as I made a beeline for the door.

"Stop!" the biker ordered. "You *din't* seen the beds in the 'ttached room." The adjoining room was a miniscule closet in which two sets of bunk beds had been crammed. The soiled mattresses had no linens.

"Look," Elise crowed, "a clubhouse!" The older girls scampered up the ladder.

"I figgered they'd like it," the biker remarked. "You git sheets at sign in."

As I sagged into defeat, I thought to ask about the pool.

"Sir, where is the swimming pool?"

"Filled it with *see'ment* during the remodel."

"No swimming pool?" I exclaimed loudly so the girls would hear. Thank God, they did.

They flew out the door chanting *we want to swim . . . you promised . . .* They couldn't have been more appropriately obnoxious if we'd rehearsed.

"They *prolly* covered a few *ho'tel* guests with *see'ment* when they remodeled," George remarked, as we squealed out of the parking lot.

Within minutes, he stopped in front of a **Buy Your Elvis Souvenirs Here** store. "I'm running in to buy Graceland tickets," he said. "You did such a great job creating this disaster, think about straightening it out, Sweetie."

Threatening bodily harm if anyone dared leave the van, I found a phone and called the Visitors Center with a gut-wrenching tale that happened to be true – four children, an exhausted husband, a marriage at stake and nowhere to go.

"Well, we do have a special facility for emergency situations," the Greeter drawled. "It's a ho'tel on the outskirts of town that is completely filled up, but during Elvis Week, and only during Elvis Week, Memphis allows them to subdivide their banquet room into small cubicles and put some fold-aways in – that's all I got."

"We'll take it," I said.

"Now, mind you, this is special for Elvis Week since it is against the Memphis Fire Code. The roll-aways are $50 per night. Check-in is at eight and check-out is at eight and there's a swimmin' pool under the escalators in the lobby."

My husband returned. "Did you find a room at Heartbreak Hotel?"

"No, but I found a cubicle with six roll-aways. Check-in is at eight."

"Cubicle? Check-in at eight? What is it, a freaking homeless shelter?"

"No, it's a Suckers' Shelter – the roll-aways are $50 each. Did you get the tickets?"

"As Elvis liked to say, I take care of business. There's a Silver ticket for $25 to tour Graceland, a Gold ticket for $40 that includes Graceland and Elvis' Auto & Cycle Museum and a $50 Platinum ticket that covers Graceland, the Auto Museum and Elvis' plane – the *Lisa Marie.*"

"You did get the Silver ticket, right?" I asked holding my breath.

"No, no, Little Woman, I splurged on Platinum. Tomorrow, all Elvis, all day."

I should just slit my wrists now, I thought.

The aroma of chlorine stung our nostrils as we entered a lobby with a guitar-shaped pool. Good 'ole boys in blue jeans and their girlfriends in Daisy Dukes were swan-diving off the escalator rails, beer cans in hand as *Don't Be Cruel* blared over the sound system.

"This isn't a pool," George shouted over the din, "it's a huge toilet. The bacterial count must be astronomical. If Elise contracts a flesh-eating disease, her parents will sue our asses off." Elise's parents were attorneys.

His point well-taken, I declared, "Girls, no swimming just yet."

"Please, please," Lia screamed in my ear, "could we at least put our feet in the water and let the fish bite our toes?"

"There are no fish in swimming pools, Lia," I snapped.

"Yes, there are," she insisted as she dragged me to the edge. "Look at the bottom!"

"Oh, my God," I gasped as I ran over to my husband who stood mesmerized by the Fellini-like scene. "You are not going to believe this. There is shit in the pool."

"Really," he said, "I'm shocked."

A bellboy with a bullhorn bellowed, "Edwards' room ready!"

"Oh, great," George said, "Jist win I was goin' ta order martinis fer the kids and let them chill by the toxic latrine."

Up the escalator and into the third floor banquet room, we found our cubicle with six cots, each covered with a white tablecloth, and the banquet room's refrigerator.

"I've never stayed in a hotel before, Mrs. Edwards," Amy announced. "Why is there such a big refrigerator in our room?"

"That's where you buy food," Gianna, who'd gotten us into this train wreck, explained. "It's filled with little bottles of whiskey and bags of peanuts. You eat as much as you want and they just add it on your bill, like magic."

Suddenly I realized we hadn't had dinner and it was ten o'clock. Since the buffet binge, the kids had only had more sugar – candy bars, ice cream and gallons of Slushees. George volunteered to get some hamburgers. He returned with $20 worth of vending machine junk food.

"You're not going to believe this, but they lock the hotel doors at 10 to keep the 'riff-raff' out."

"Mr. Edwards," Elise, the future mini-litigator piped up, "tell them we demand to get our suitcases so we can put on our pajamas."

"Oh, no this will be more fun," I interrupted, "We're going to eat Doritos and Twizzlers and then sleep in our clothes!"

"Yippeee," Elise shouted. "When I tell my Mom and Dad what we did on this vacation they're not going to believe it!"

"After Elise's parents finish with us, we'll lose our kids to the Department of Children and Family Services," George commented, "and I'm not going to appeal."

"Let's try to get some sleep," I said, confident he'd relent and appeal after a few months.

At six George announced it was time to rise and shine. No tooth-brushing, no showering – no dressing, for that matter, just breakfast and head over to Graceland. Arriving at eight, we found a huge crowd ahead of us.

"Probably everyone comes here first," my husband figured. "Let's start at the airplane instead."

After an hour and a half in the plane line, we entered the cockpit of the *Lisa Marie*, Elvis' beloved jet named after his only child. He must have decorated the plane about the time his drug use was spinning out of control. Only an hallucinogenic could have prompted 24 karat gold-flecked sinks and gold-plated seat belts. WARNING-DO NOT TOUCH! signs were plastered everywhere. Suddenly alarms and bells were going off and security was rushing the plane as though a sniper was holed up in the fur-walled bathroom. Lia was not in sight. Sure enough, she had jumped on Elvis' bed. Within minutes, we were escorted off the *Lisa Marie*. Being kicked off the plane suited me just fine.

We stood in line for only an hour at the Graceland Auto Museum to view the Pink Cadillac, Ferrari, John Deere tractor and motorcycles. This time the temptation proved to be too much for Gianna who climbed onto the King's Harley when our backs were turned and, again, security force promptly took care of business. We were back in the broiling sun before we'd even seen his tractor.

Sensing I was near meltdown, George suggested a bit of shopping while he stood guard over our little terrorists outside. I ducked into the Elvis Store where I found a colossal supply of ashtrays, lamps, guitars, lawn mowers, teddy bears, teapots, brassieres – all with The Great One's Coat of Arms, a lightning bolt. The only thing not on display was a replica of the toilet seat he was sitting on the night he fell off the stool and died on the bathroom floor.

As I exited the store, I found Gianna wailing – she wanted to buy an Elvis guitar, Elise pouting – she needed an Elvis wig – and the other two arguing.

"I think they're hungry," my husband said. "Let's go to the Elvis Café."

They ordered Elvis' favorite – a deep-fried sandwich of bananas, peanut butter and marshmallow fluff with a side of French fries and a deep-fried pickle. The big girls shared a piece of Sweet Potato Cream Cheese Pie. Lia and Elise had Moon Pies.

We waddled over to Graceland where the line of mutants from another planet snaked around the block – seventy-five year old ingenues with lightning bolts tattooed on their breasts, dudes in high heels and make-up, a man in SCUBA diving gear and a lady with a raccoon on a leash to name but a few. Taking up the rear, Lia threw the mother of all tantrums – "I hate Elvis! This is the dumbest vacation I ever went on in my life! This is all Gianna's fault! I am sick of Elvis and his stupid songs!"

"Calm her down," George hissed. "People are staring."

"Staring? *At us*?" I ranted. "They're staring *at us*?"

"Mom," Lia, having tantrumed out, called to me, "what does 'Elvis sucks elephant dick' mean?" I spun around to read the graffiti that completely covered the five-foot stone wall surrounding America's second most visited historic residence after The White House. Amy ran over with an eye-witness report. "Mrs. Edwards, a guy dressed like Elvis just peed on the wall to clean off a space so he could write something."

"Amy, maybe it was Elvis peeing," Gianna suggested. "That lady over there in the nightgown told me Elvis is not dead."

I could not fathom what I'd done in a past life to deserve this. At last we entered the hallowed Graceland.

Saddam Hussein had nothing on Elvis' home decor. The "jungle" den, the billiards room, the TV room where Elvis shot out the screen once when he didn't like the program, the gun room where he practiced target shooting, past his parents' bedroom, into the kitchen where he'd made his 'heart-attack on a plate' snacks – we saw it all. We ogled his trophies, Gold Records, jewelry, costumes and awards. The only sacred site off limits was the infamous bathroom.

The tour ended in the Meditation Garden where speakers, hidden under bushes, blared *How Great Thou Art.* A bit to the left of the swimming pool, flanked by the tombs of his parents, Vernon and Gladys, Elvis rests.

His autopsy revealed he'd ingested at least 10 different drugs, including morphine, within the last 24 hours of his life. I wondered how he got along with so few.

Under the Sea

The resort manager welcomed us to the B of the ABC Dutch Islands. Aruba is the capitol of wind-surfing, he raved. Curacao is famous for its rum, but Bonaire, ahhh, Bonaire is the dive capital of the western hemisphere. "We may not have sites to see or stores to shop," he continued, "but it does not matter because you can be under the sea twenty-four hours a day and never see the same reef twice. "

There would be dawn dives, sunrise dives, morning dives, lunch dives and too many more dives to mention before the midnight dive, our host explained. I knew my husband would only skip a dive when he was detoxing, and, during those brief periods, he would be sleeping or cleaning his equipment.

My spouse changes planes six times and travels through five time zones on the other side of the International Date Line in search of thumb-sized crustaceans, all while lugging a hundred pounds of gear.

A satellite flies over his dive boat once every twelve hours allowing a five minute window to reach out and touch someone.

"HI, I'M IN *&^%$*^&*#@*^>."

"CAN YOU HEAR ME?"

"BARELY. SPEAK *&%$*^&%&^$."

"HOW ARE *&%$#&^*&^*@!&."

"ARE YOU HAVING *&^*^%$*^&$."

The line goes dead. A couple of 3 a.m.'s later my husband and I have the same *conversation*.

He smushes into a girdle-tight wet suit several times a day, island hops where the natives have never seen a white man, and returns home totally worn out.

My husband is a SCUBA fanatic, and I just don't get it.

By nine-years-old, he'd developed his diving obsession, neither knowing nor caring about technical procedures or safety precautions. On our first date he rhapsodized about Lloyd Bridges, Sea Hunt, and Jacques Cousteau. I didn't pay much attention because I was busy falling in love.

He traded the ocean for the University of Chicago and marriage so I thought his passion would burned out, but it only smoldered and reignited when he quit smoking. *Wouldn't a dive trip be a wonderful incentive to stay the course, I thought? Were there travel agents who specialized in dive trips?*

Soon I was explaining to the owner of Ultimate Dive Travel, about my husband's long ago passion, and the need for a special reward.

"Any trips to the Keys?" I asked. "He grew up in Florida."

"How special is this guy?"

"Very special," I assured, "the best."

"Well, if he's really special, and takes a refresher course, I have the trip of a lifetime going out three months from today."

Without further thought, I provided the digits on my American Express.

That loving gesture began annual voyages to Palau, Lhaviyani Atoll, Wakatobi and other unpronounceable destinations despite having the Shedd Aquarium in our backyard.

Once, tired of the *you don't know what you're missing . . . try it just once* badgering, I snorkeled in Lake Michigan. Water flooded my breathing tube, I saw a shark; I panicked. *Don't ever ask me to risk my life again,* I warned my husband.

So that's why it was stupid of me to accompany the *I'd Rather Be Diving Club* to Bonaire.

Perhaps I bought into it because we hadn't vacationed together for a long time – my opting for Venice when he set off for Vanuatu – then again I may have been swayed by 85 degrees vs. February in Chicago, whatever, I signed on.

After a couple of stopovers, we arrived at a Third World airport where the Customs Agents obviously smoked any confiscated ganja, and couldn't care less if you had a bomb in your flip-flops. Thirty-eight divers and two heretics scrambled to find the pick-up trucks – one per couple. The trucks were stick shift, but first gear was all we needed since paved roads were nonexistent.

The other non-diver was a wife who had a much better attitude than I. Either she actually found this escapade fun, which I doubt because she seemed normal, or, she'd learned to fake it. Our good time consisted of visits to the bakery or barren supermercado bucking down the road in first-gear. Even swimming was maddening – kick too hard, and you whacked a goggled, flippered creature exploring just below the surface.

After six days of this scenario, I selfishly asked my husband if we might spend a bit of time together. "Honey," I said, when I caught him awake on land, "do you think maybe you could skip a dive, and we could do something fun?"

"Like what?" he stammered, terrified he was going to have to interact with something that had no fins.

"Well, we could go to the bakery and get a donut or the grocery store and have a Coke," I suggested.

"Which place is closer?" he asked. "I don't have a lot of time to play around."

"Look, I'm beginning to feel like Robinson Crusoe marooned on this Island of Despair. The only conversation I've had has been with that freaking parrot at the front desk. I can't even swim with the dolphins because the entire ocean is clogged with creatures in black dominatrix suits," I wailed, causing the geckos in the room to skitter for cover.

"Simmer down," my husband said. "Do you want everyone on the island to hear you ranting?"

"No one will hear me – they're all under water. I can understand why those kids in *Lord of the Flies* descended into savagery – they had nothing else to do on that god-forsaken island! I feel like Piggy."

"Okay, okay I get the picture. I'll borrow Bill's laptop, and we can look at his reef shots together."

"You're joking, right?" I said, on the verge of going for his throat. "I don't want to look at slides nor do I want to discuss bioluminescence nor do I give a shit about nitrox psychosis," I screamed.

"Well would you like to SNUBA?" he asked. "It's a cross between snorkeling and SCUBA. You go a little deeper than snorkeling because you breathe through a hose that's tethered to a compressor on an overhead raft," he said, with a how's-that-for-a-treat look.

"You have got to be effing kidding me," I said, appalled at his suggestion. "I'd rather stick pins in my eyeballs."

"Where's your sense of humor, Little Woman? If you hadn't launched into one of your epic tantrums, I'd have told you that I planned to take you kayaking in the mangroves tomorrow. I'm sacrificing my afternoon dive."

I knew he'd made up this plan on the spot because he feared for his life, but at least I stood a chance of taking a few good memories from Gilligan's Island after all.

The next afternoon found us at the Bonaire Marine Park Visitors Center being in-serviced " . . . by an ecologist who will briefly interrupt the gentle trip with explanations of the interrelationships that exist between the mangroves and the sea." We were given a bottle of water, a viewer that looked like a cheerleader's megaphone with a glass bottom and a kayak built for two. After the interminable orientation we were off with our guide, Doortje, the Dutch Amazon Queen of the Ecosphere.

As we monkey-pulled ourselves on the overhead mangrove roots through a tube-like tunnel, Doortje lectured. Swarms of mosquitoes were biting my eyelids, flying up my nostrils and clogging my ear canals causing me to only catch snippets of Eco-Queen's litany of DO NOT'S. "**Do not** go into the sea-beds! **Do not** litter! **Do not** touch the landscape! **Do not** speak loudly!" Doortje warned. "This is the most endangered eco-scape on the planet! Our primary purpose is to avoid, at all costs, damage to the fragile environment!"

My spouse maneuvered us through the maze of tangled ceiling roots out to the open sea where I, for the first time, thought this could be fun. I was wrong.

Within the hour, we violated all of Doortje's **DO NOT'S** because she failed to mention that, *only under normal circumstances,* are kayaks stable platforms.

As the kayaks circled the jellyfish lagoon – *"Careful here, Doortje cautioned, because multiple jelly stings will put you in shock."* – I became aware that I was working awfully hard; I suspected my husband was not pulling his weight. Not wanting to turn around and wobble the *stable platform,* I yelled to George's favorite buddy diver, "Bill, is he paddling? I feel like I'm doing all the work, and this thing is unbalanced or something." "Oh, he's paddling fine," Bill assured. By now the kayak was shuddering. "Anne," I shouted to Bill's wife, my new best friend, "I can't look behind me, this kayak is really shaky. Tell me the truth, is he really paddling back there?"

Before she could answer, the kayak rolled over. When I surfaced, I heard the Amazon screeching, "The eco-system! Don't put your feet down in the sea grass. Get back in the kayak! Jump into the kayak!"

"Doortje," I sputtered, "the water is five feet deep, I'm five feet tall. How do you get back in to one of these things?"

"Use your arm muscles," she ordered. "You're destroying the eco-system!"

"Screw the eco-system – something is snapping at my legs," I screamed.

"You are ruining a fish spawning habitat. You could be arrested!"

"If the Ocean Patrol can pull me out, I'll be glad to go to jail," I snarled, trying to float to keep from stepping on copulating barracuda.

"Use your shoulders! Flip your body into the kayak!" She was wild with horror.

I called in all my God chits in exchange for a supernatural jolt of adrenaline. My husband was no help, trying to yank me up by the straps of my swimsuit which did nothing but give me a freaking wedgie.

"Please don't touch me," I snapped, "you've already done way more than enough to make this trip memorable."

Then, with a plea to St. Jude, I grabbed the side of the kayak, and with every ounce of strength I had in my marshmallow biceps, I hoisted my butt from the sacred waters. I lay contorted over the kayak like a salted pretzel baking in the scorching sun. The rest of the dive club applauded, knowing they'd just witnessed a miracle. My agile husband, relieved, hopped up, and heaved his knee over the side of the boat, but, alas, his other knee didn't quite make it.

For the second time in as many minutes, I was eye-to-eye with sting-rays. I vowed that, if I made it to land, my husband's next air-tank would be filled with carbon monoxide.

Doortje was apoplectic. "Your paddle! Your paddle! You are wrecking the sanctuary," she bleated, enraged that I was destroying her sacred ecosystem. "Where is your water bottle?!"

Where is my water bottle? This bitch is screeching about a water bottle?

"Never mind my water bottle, Doortje, my Crocs fell off," I said, referring to the platypus-looking rubber sandals that were all the rage. "My Crocs fell off – they must be trapped in the sea grass," I taunted, just to really push her over the edge.

"Crocs? Crocs! Oh my God, Crocs," she screamed as she leaped into the brine.

She surfaced with one Croc. "I got it," she crowed, and returned to the sea bed to find the other. She surfaced triumphantly waving the second sandal, as though she was some kind of Champion Rocky, and vaulted into her kayak.

She glared at me like I was not even worthy of the lowest slot on her stupid ass eco-food chain. "Get in the kayak," she growled, "and don't dare fall out again!"

Don't dare fall out again? Don't dare fall out again? Here I was a salt-encrusted codfish, feeling like Lot's wife, and this lunatic was acting as though I deliberately somersaulted into her aquarium?

Well, I decided, it takes one psycho-bitch to know one. I'd make Doortje wish she'd been finished off by a Great White while she was on the Croc search.

"No, Doortje, I am not getting back on the Titanic," I shrieked. "You do what I say or I'll put my feet down in this freaking fish tank, and wipe out your entire eco-habitat!"

She saw I was a woman possessed.

"Turn your kayak over to me now! I'm paddling alone – get out of that boat," I roared. "I'm not spending all day flipping in and out of this Lusitania! You get into this piece of fiberglass shit, and he hops in with you–no more of this tandem crap for me – I'm paddlin' solo!" I raved. "You two can spend forever tipping over that goddamned dinghy for all I care! Now move it – get the hell out!"

Doortje gaped as though I was Lizzie Borden in a life-jacket. She hopped out of that damn kayak so fast she almost lost her safari hat.

"Now hand over my sandals," I ordered. "Maybe if I click my flippin' Crocs, I can at least get to Kansas."

Is There a Problem Officer?

The drama always starts the same. I'll be driving along, engrossed in some NPR report on the Cretaceous mastodon's influence on the nuclear industry, when suddenly I'm distracted by screaming sirens and the flashing lights of a squad car tailgating me. I pull over to get out of harm's way only to be shocked that I am the target. The officer moseys over and, without even asking if I am running late or need to be somewhere, demands my license.

"Is there a problem, Officer?" I ask, handing over the precious piece of plastic.

"You were doing 60 miles per hour in a 45 zone, Miss. I'll be right back. Stay in your car."

He heads back to his squad, and starts scribbling. I never understand why he expresses no interest in the reason for my alleged speeding; why he won't give me a pass if I promise to slow down. Why are they always in a hurry to write up a citation in triplicate? They never take a second to listen to a plausible explanation or care that this ticket might precipitate a divorce.

"This pink copy is stapled to your license which will be returned to you when you appear in Traffic Court on your appointed court date; yellow copy is to drive on 'til you get your license back. Drive safely and obey the law!" And, poof, the misogynist is gone.

It is common knowledge that a lot of policemen, who are mentally damaged by their mothers, target females out of malice and revenge and, as a result, I get pulled over regularly for nonsense. I am sick of gender profiling.

This prejudice could interfere with my career; in fact, it could stop me cold. Three moving violations within a 12-month period would push me out of the driver's seat so I have always challenged the tickets in Traffic Court. For the most part I drive in the Chicago area, Land of Corrupt Judges, where murderers routinely walk free, so I always feel it is worth a shot.

My well-connected husband knows many political insiders, who could change the course of events with a mere phone call, but he refuses to intervene on my behalf. His ridiculous rationalization is that to do so would only encourage my reckless behavior and wanton disrespect for the law. The result is that again and again I rub shoulders with lawless bikers and menacing thugs in the halls of so-called justice while trying to protect my livelihood.

"I am so sick of Officer Friendly wasting his time, and mine, with these unwarranted citations when he should be out catching rapists. What is their problem?" I lamented to my husband.

"Your license telegraphs your reckless driving history," he replied. "The cop doesn't even have to look at it, he just feels the staple holes – it's like reading Braille. He knows immediately you're a serial speeder and a chronic pain in the ass."

"A person is innocent until proven guilty; I have Constitutional rights, you know."

"Do you see what I mean about being a pain in the ass?"

After I learned of the cop's unfair Braille advantage, I went to the Illinois Department of Motor Vehicles, another graveyard of corruption, and had my *stolen license* replaced. However, the staple holes always resprouted, and I didn't want to become a fixture at the DMV so, at my wit's end, I devised the *pregnancy.*

If I got a ticket for going less than 15 miles over the speed limit, I'd wear a maternity dress to court. I almost always walked out a free woman.

More than 15 miles over the limit, I'd wear the maternity schmata plus borrow a friend's poorly behaved child – there was never a shortage of candidates. The judge would note my being in a family way dragging this rambunctious munchkin around so I was usually excused lickety-split.

If the infraction was particularly egregious, I'd toddle over in the maternity dress hauling a few more obnoxious trolls.

One day in a suburban court, where they mix traffic violators with murderers willy-nilly, an attractive, well-dressed man sat down next to me.

"Pardon me, but what's a nice girl like you doing in a place like this?" he asked.

"I wonder the same thing every time I wind up here. I don't belong with these gangbangers and criminals, but I refuse to pay a shyster lawyer to represent me so I'm stuck. Why are you here?"

"I'm a shyster lawyer," he said. "So are you married? Where you from? What's your name?"

"I'm not really into twenty questions. Let's leave the interrogation to the judge, okay?"

"Sorry, but you look familiar. Are you from around here? Who's your husband?"

I told him and, as often happens in big city/small town Chicago, he knew my spouse.

"Your husband," he exclaimed, sotto voiced, "could have had this taken care of with a simple phone call. A woman like you doesn't belong here with this pond scum, not to mention in your condition. This is absurd!"

"You're right," I said, "but he will not lift a finger on my behalf. He's like Chillingworth in the **Scarlet Letter;** *she must pay for her mistakes . . ."*

Just then the bailiff called my name. "How do you plead?" the judge thundered. Suddenly a hand from behind grabbed my shoulder, and the man attached to the hand, boomed, "Your Honor, my client pleads not guilty!"

"Dismissed!" gaveled the judge. "Next case!"

Now, I subscribe to the Henry VI school of thought that we should just kill all the lawyers, but, in this instance, I appreciated the intervention.

"Lady Justice took pity on me," I said. "Thanks for the help."

"Don't mention it," he laughed. "My judges get big Christmas presents. Oh, and by the way, tell your husband he owes Big Lou a favor."

When I relayed the message to my husband he said he didn't owe anybody, anything, "Never have, never will. And you'd better be a little more discerning about your acquaintances – that lawyer is a crook."

Not a year later, I read about Mr. Shyster being sent to Statesville for money laundering and bribery, but he wasn't the only one in a jam.

Judge X had ruled *not guilty* in one of my more complicated cases involving an *alleged illegal U-turn.* I explained that I'd planned to make a left turn, but that my steering wheel was overly sensitive, and spun me into an involuntary U-turn. Several months later, I again stood in front of Judge X for *allegedly running a red light.* As I waddled toward the bench, His Honor's eyes bulged.

"Mrs. E," he said, "The court does not wish to cause you undue stress while you are still on stork watch so I am going to continue your case until you return with your newborn's birth certificate."

"That bastard knows I can't deliver," I fumed to my husband. "Maybe now is the time to start our family, and call his bluff."

"Are you nuts? You've outdone the Frilled Shark's gestation period of three and a half years, for god's sake. It's too bad that Big Lou's in prison and can't be on your legal team to explain your years of hopping around the judicial system with a bun in the oven. A bun, I might add, that has been baking for at least a decade."

"You're right," I conceded. "It's time for the pregnancy thing to end. I'll show the Judge a car accident report, and tell him that I suffered complications. I'll wear a black dress and a veil like Jackie Kennedy."

"Do that," my husband said, "and I guarantee you'll wind up in an orange jumpsuit sitting next to your buddy Lou."

There was a pregnant pause.

Saving Her from Neverland

"I'm working an eight-hour day next Thursday."

"That's good," I said, intent on reading the latest issue of **Vanity Fair**.

"Mom, you didn't hear what I said," my twenty-something persisted. "I'm not working my usual three hour shift – he scheduled me for an *eight-hour day*."

"I heard you, Honey. Eight hours a week won't hurt you."

"Won't hurt? You think that's a good thing – being a go-fer for my Art teacher for eight hours straight? Did you ever hear of throbbing feet or varicose veins?"

"Yes, Sweetheart, I have heard of the tortuous blood vessels, but you can get saline shots, the veins collapse, and you're not disfigured."

"Not disfigured? Is that your yardstick? I can work until I'm disfigured? Don't you care that I could get scoliosis and need to have a rod put in my back?"

Count to ten, hold your tongue, 25 is the new 15 . . .

"As I understand it, Tinkerbell, scoliosis develops in early adolescence so I think you're out of the woods. And I do care about spinal curvatures and, more importantly, I care about you."

"Well, it sure doesn't sound like it. Aren't you worried that I could get a collapsed uterus from being on my legs all day and never be able to bear children? That no man will ever want to marry someone who's physically flawed – that I could die a spinster painting landscapes in a nursing home?"

Her losses were escalating so fast I feared she'd have nothing left for the final chapter of her book **I Am a Prima Donna**.

"Yes, Angel, I do worry. I worry that if you don't get over your aversion to an eight-hour day, you'll be living at home until you're menopausal. That, my love, is a very scary thought."

"Mother, you are heartless. I can't believe you support child labor."

"Child labor? I was married at your age, for God's sake. It's time you joined the real world."

"Don't try to change the subject, Mom. This isn't about just one eight-hour day. I'm also on the schedule for eight hours next Thursday."

"Eight hours next week too?" I said, lapsing into my Dolly Parton voice. "Well ain't that sad. You should just put the paramedics on alert right now in case you pass out from fatigue."

"You're being sarcastic, Mother. Go ahead mock me, laugh at me all you want, but I'm under a great deal of pressure. If I'm chained to a job, I can't have a social life. Michelangelo probably had a better social life than I do even though he was gay and had to be in the closet."

"Look, I know eight hours a week cramps your style but, and you need to sit down for this, many people work eight hours a day on a regular basis, back to back, five days a week."

"I'm well aware of that, but I don't intend to be a slave."

"Slave? What are you talking about? A forty-hour work week is not fun, but living in a cardboard box is not exactly a blast either."

"You're suggesting I'm going to be living under a bridge? Thanks for the vote of confidence. When I finish my degree, Sarah, Kirsten and I plan to share an apartment in the John Hancock Center."

The Hancock Center? I didn't want to disillusion her by mentioning that, on their combined salaries, they couldn't afford a closet in the skyscraper.

"Interesting, but first you really should graduate."

"Don't you think I know that? That's why I'm trying to concentrate on my studies, but I can't do that if I'm always working."

"Always working? Eight hours a week? Are you serious?"

"Yes, I'm serious. Eight hours in one day is challenging because I really don't like my job. I mean working in the art studio is okay, but it's not my passion."

"Passion? Well if you'd quit changing majors like that Lohan girl changes rehabs, you just might finish up and follow your bliss. One semester you're majoring in Art Design, the next in Painting, then Art & Media Management, whatever that is. You probably won't believe this, Snow White, but some kids finish college in four years."

"You should be glad I'm staying in the School of Fine Arts. My friend, Ian, switched from Electrical Engineering to Dance. He transferred from Princeton to Juilliard in his senior year and he had a full-ride at Princeton."

"Well his parents must be brain-damaged to allow that. If you switch majors one more time, I swear your father is going to say *teacher or nurse – take your pick.*"

"Mom, I could never be a nurse. They're on their feet eight hours a day. It's a very stressful job. I want a job where I can relax."

Was I watching a rerun of an ancient TV show where unsuspecting victims were placed in ridiculous situations while a hidden camera recorded their reactions? Surely someone was going to jump out and shout **Smile, You're on Candid Camera**.

"Relax? Sweetie, I have another news flash for you. One goes to a spa to relax. One goes to work so she can buy food, keep a roof over her head – you know, the finer things in life."

"Yes, and many have heart-attacks before they're forty or they die of mesothelioma from breathing in coal dust."

"Well, you needn't worry about that. Last time I applied they weren't hiring at the coal mines."

"And that's another reason I'm in no hurry to graduate. There are no decent jobs out there. I should rush through college to flip hamburgers? I don't think so. Are you aware there is a recession out there?"

"Really? You're kidding? I thought your dad lost our retirement nest egg in Las Vegas."

"Don't worry about retirement, Mom. If you fall on hard times, you can count on me to catch you. That's why I want to go to Florence to get my master's degree."

Bless her – her heart was in the right place – it was her head that was in Neverland. The vision of being caught in a safety net that was one huge hole flashed before me, but it was immediately replaced by flares at the words Florence and master's degree in the same sentence.

"Florence? In Italy? You're joking, right?" *Please, God, let the Candid Camera man jump out now.* "Tell me you're kidding."

"No, I have to get my master's degree – a B.A. in Art is practically worthless. Do you remember when we were in Italy and I met Gianmarco? He suggested I do graduate work in Art Restoration at the Florence Academy. He said you can set your own hours. Can you imagine what it would be like to restore a Caravaggio?"

"Caravaggio?" I was setting some kind of record for responding to comments with a single word of incredulity. "Caravaggio? Did that Gian-gigolo tell you how to finance this adventure?"

"Mother, you-are-putting-a-*price*-on-passion?" she wailed, as though I'd suggested she sell her firstborn, forgetting that she'd never bear children due to her fallen uterus. "That is soooo cynical. You *follow* a passion, not *finance* a passion!"

"You know, Cinderella, unless you find a glass slipper in your bottomless closet, you might have to put in a few eight-hour days in order to *follow AND finance* your passion. Even Michelangelo had to make tough choices. Sculpting was his passion – he considered the Sistine Chapel project a huge distraction, but he needed to pay his bills."

"That's exactly my point," she said. "Michelangelo compromised, and he was chained to scaffolding for the next forty-years. What was he thinking?"

Death Valley Spa

For the past four months, my friend Ellen and I'd been able to cobble together daily hour long walks, aided by the fact that she was in the midst of a contentious divorce and dissecting her almost-ex made the time fly. I was on a roll with these treks, and I was reluctant to jeopardize this long aspired-to accomplishment by accompanying my husband on a business trip to Scottsdale. I feared that without the almost-divorcee keeping my feet to the pavement, I'd slack off.

"I can't believe you're not interested in escaping a minus ten degree wind chill," he marveled. "People do walk in Arizona, you know."

"I know, but I'm afraid I'll be tempted to just sit by the pool and not move my butt."

"There's a resort that adjoins the desert. You can walk the Sonora trails, I'll golf."

By the end of the month we were in Scottsdale, and the morning after our arrival I was at the concierge desk.

"Did you want to walk Trail A or B?" the concierge asked.

"Which is easier?"

"Trail A varies from one to three shoes. Trail B is quite challenging," she explained. "One shoe is the least demanding, five shoes requires a lot of stamina. Don't forget to take water and a hat. It gets hot out there."

"I'm not going to be out long," I said, distracted by her spectacular turquoise jewelry. "I love your squash blossom necklace."

"Thank you, it was my grandmother's. If you're into Native American jewelry, you'll be in heaven in Arizona. Here's a map of all the jewelry shops in the Old Town area where you can do some serious shopping."

I stuck the map in my pocket. "Well right now I need to get some serious exercise."

"You came to the right place. I'm not a hiker, but our guests rave about the trails. Enjoy yourself."

"I will, and I'd better get moving if I want to check out the Navajo silversmiths this afternoon. I'll pass on the five shoe route; just point me to the beginner's trail."

"Go behind the restaurant, between the tennis courts, past the gate, through the tunnel and you will emerge on Trail A. Have fun!"

Within minutes, I crossed into God's country – a landscape at once both brawny and delicate. Muted terra cotta, vibrant purples, and hazy greens stippled the scene. This was not the desert of pyramid fame, where I'd scorched my soles in the Sahara sand, but the desert of the Good, the Bad and the Ugly – the majestic stomping ground of Geronimo.

Nothing prepared a girl from the Prairie State for this vista.

I pictured Butch Cassidy galloping over the saguaro-studded hills, Wyatt Earp hunting down cattle rustlers, John Wayne lassoing varmints. This was desperado territory.

Setting forth, I almost twisted my ankle on my first step into the wild. *Be careful in these flimsy sandals,* I reminded myself. *This trail is not asphalt.* I noted a Visitors Center and a BE PREPARED sign, that smacked of overkill with its million suggestions obviously written by a Boy Scout working on his Wilderness Survival Badge. For starters, he suggested a whistle, water, compass, map, knife, mirror, matches, candles and a blanket. Matches, around tumbleweed? Water, with no porta-pottys? A blanket in this furnace? Ridiculous. Besides, I was going for a walk; it wasn't as though I was Sacagawea on an expedition with Lewis and Clark.

I marched onto the one-shoe trail, the piece-of-cake one, where I'd planned to walk for a half-hour and then turn back, all the while keeping my eye on the Visitors Center. Every so often, I murmured good morning to a jogger or a dog-walker. "Oh, she's adorable," I gushed over a puppy who sported saddle-bags and a water bottle. I passed a few Girl Scouts laughing and a woman, on her cell phone, bleating, "Snowing again? . . . Well, it's absolutely gorgeous here." At every turn, I encountered desertscapes I'd only seen in movies in which cowboys fell in love with Indian maidens, and white men smoked peace pipes with the Chief. Images of gun-slingers, runaway stagecoaches and saloon hussies ran through my head.

Each time I thought to turn back, I discovered a new distraction – a giant cactus pockmarked with bird-pecked holes, a mysterious rock pile, a jackrabbit zigzagging out of harm's way. Moseying from pillar to post, it occurred to me that I'd not passed a human for awhile, and the sun was bleaching out the aubergine highlights I got at the Buzz Salon just before we left Chicago. It was time to get out of Dodge, and fast.

I did a one-eighty, but when I turned around, the shiny roof of the Visitors Center was nowhere in sight.

You're a little off course – no big deal. You curved to the right when you entered, so just hang to the left. Then I got a bit nervous. *You should've worn a hat. Maybe I shouldn't have worn velour; I'm melting. Where the hell did the Center go? Are these buffalo footprints? Do buffalo bite?*

An hour later, I knew I was in trouble.

Nothing looks familiar. Don't shed a tear, you'll dehydrate. Do they have desert rangers? Keep your wits about you. If only I could see a landmark like Sears Tower. I should have brought a knife or a mirror like the sign said, but what was I supposed to do with a mirror anyway? Too late now, you're toast.

Just as I was about to gather rocks to spell out "farewell," I spotted a metal marker with an arrow pointing to Trail 306 and another to Trail 100 in the opposite direction.

What's with the trail numbers? Where was the one-shoe trail? The U.S. Wildlife Service lures visitors into Death Valley, and can't even post an EXIT arrow? Just choose a trail – you have a fifty-fifty chance of being right. Turn to the left. You are not lost; you've just strayed a bit off the beaten path.

Before me was a two-foot high, log-shaped cactus lying on its side.

And then it clicked. *You-are-lost. You are so lost. If you'd passed this heat-stroked, phallic symbol on the way in, you'd have remembered – it looks exactly like Ellen's description of her husband's erectile dysfunction.*

I scanned for a human – a nomad, a migrant, a wrangler, even a gold prospector, anyone. I caught sight of a jogger.

"Stop! Stop!" I shouted, afraid he might not see me in the withering inferno. "Please help me," I begged. "I'm lost!"

"Relax. You're just turned around. Where do you want to go?"

"To my hotel – I'm a tourist."

"Really?" Just what I needed, a condescending savior, but I was in no position to call him on his attitude. "Where's your map?"

"I only have this map of the jewelry stores in Old Town."

"A map of jewelry stores?" he asked with a *there's no cure for stupid* look. "Alright, let's get you oriented. You see the sun overhead? It's a bit to our left because it's still early, so that's east. Now because it's late February it makes a bit of a wider arc as it crosses the sky to the . . . to the . . .?"

"To the other side?"

"Well, yes, but we call the other side the west," he said, taking a long draw on a tube connected to a CamelBak HydroFlo contraption strapped to his back.

I wanted to tell Mr. Professor that I hated Geography and Astronomy or wherever the hell you learn about the Big Dipper and the solar system, but I didn't want him to think I was direction-impaired.

"Now pay attention. This will always be east, that will always be north and this will always be south," he said, pointing to the three directions. "Where did you enter the canyon?"

"From the tunnel."

"Seventh Street or Seventh Avenue?"

"I have no idea. How many blocks is it to the Visitors Center?"

"Blocks? How many blocks?" he repeated, as though he'd caught me tossing beer cans on the trail. "Where are you from?"

"Chicago."

"Ooookay, so, now you know north and south. Do you see that dip between those two mountains, kind of looks like a camel's back?"

This whole town is camelback crazy, Camelback Estates, Camelback Country Club, Camelback Condo . . .

He interrupted my thoughts. "You're not paying attention. That's how we got lost, isn't it?"

Whose 'we,' Tonto? I'm the one who's lost, and right now I could be shopping for a turquoise bracelet in Old Town.

"Stay on this trail, and keep heading toward the dip," he continued. "Pretend you're a soccer ball rolling . . ."

Now I cut him off. "Dude, I understand sports only slightly less than I understand the solar system."

"Okay, never mind. Do you see that white dot way down there?"

"The trash bag on the cactus?"

"That's NOT a trash bag. It's a woman in a white robe meditating. Head towards her. Follow the curve and you'll come to the iron railing you passed on your way in. You do remember the railing, right?"

"Yes, I remember the black railing."

"It's green," he said. "Grab onto it, it leads to the tunnel. By the way, your cell phone has a GPS."

"I only know how to make calls and text." He took a deep breath as though I'd just declared I was a saturated-fat addict.

"Well, next time, let's hope you come prepared," he said with a fake smile.

"Oh, I don't think there'll be a next time," I said. "I'm pretty sure I'm done with the desert."

I could tell he thought that wasn't a bad idea. "You'll be okay now; just don't leave the trail." He took another swallow from his CamelHydroFlo and trotted off.

"Thanks a lot," I shouted after him. "You saved my life!"

He wasn't my kind of guy, but he did rescue me. I could've run into a Peyote-munching gangbanger marauding the happy hunting ground. A century from now, a Boy Scout could have stumbled on my little carcass and wondered why a fossil was wearing a tiny jogging suit.

At last, I spotted the shimmery roof of the Visitors Center. I texted Ellen.

GOT TRND ROUND IN DESERT. CLOSE CALL.

She responded within a second.

OMG! U CLD HV DIED!! FRND LOST IN PALM SPRGS DESERT OVRNGHT. SNAKES SCORPIONS ALMST FROZ 2 DEATH! MORN FOUND CAR PKG LOT ONLY BLOCK AWAY! B CARFL!

That was the straw that, and I couldn't believe I had to say it, broke the freakin' camel's back. Next time I want a desert fix, I'll order Blazing Saddles from Netflix.

Grave Sight

When I was eight years old, my Italian family's field trips to Mt. Carmel cemetery were mandatory pilgrimages of faith and tradition. While my sister and I picked dandelions and played he loves me, he loves me not, my parents pulled weeds and trimmed the grass and my brother sorted out the family tree. I saw the occasional bunny hop past, as we did our own version of grave-hopping.

It was only natural then that when a friend said, "I forgot today is Mother's Day so I have to cancel our walk and run to the cemetery," I considered joining her. But then I remembered that my mother considered trips to the graveyard a waste of time, and she'd be more pleased if I got some writing done.

As a little girl, I remembered checking out the mini-mausoleums, Lilliputian houses of the wealthy, that were mixed in with the tombstones of the less well-off and the tiny stone "pillows" of those not inclined to go for broke. If the people buried in the little granite houses are so rich I asked my mom, why didn't they build bigger houses? They don't need a lot of room, she said, they're not going to be doing much in the way of entertaining.

Mother's Day and Father's Day, and sometimes Memorial Day, too, would find us on our knees in Section H, Block 12, Lot 115 praying for the poor souls though I was pretty sure they had all gone straight to heaven. Just wait 'til I climb down from this stool my mother would threaten from her polishing perch when my brother would burst into his creepy Boy Scout ditty . . . *the worms go in, the worms go out, the worms play pinochle in your mouth.* At some point my sister and I would put in some pout-time because, despite his inappropriate singing, my brother was the only one who got to lug the sprinkling can to and from the graves because the spigot was down by the road. But even with all of the great adventures, I didn't really like visiting the dead. The looks on my mom's and dad's faces always made me sad, and I would inevitably wipe a sniffle on my sleeve.

While she shined the little ceramic portraits of her mother, father and brother with her hanky, she'd admonish me out of dad's earshot, "Don't cry," even though I'd see teardrops dribbling down her own cheeks when she leaned over to kiss my Nonna's picture. "Daddy likes to follow this ritual out of respect, but if you honor people when they're alive, buy them flowers when they can smell them, you don't need to waste time on your knees at a gravesite. Besides," she'd add, "they're in your heart. There's nothing here."

Ever the pragmatist, she seized learning moments as we tip-toed through the tombstones. "Brush up on your math," she'd say, "subtract their birth dates from the date they died. Do you see that Nonno died in 1918 – he died in the Great Flu Epidemic. Look it up when we get home." So I wasn't surprised when she chose a very non-traditional, but ever so practical, exit strategy.

Her decision to be cremated shocked those who needed to know – they'd be deprived of the sacred tradition of trooping to Mt. Carmel on every freaking holiday with a sprinkling can – but she blew off the criticism.

There were no more available plots at the family gravesite where my father was buried, and she wanted to be with him – moving him was out of the question, too macabre and expensive. She opted for cremation, and her urn would be entombed over his coffin. I wonder if the fact that she'd be on top factored into her decision. I imagine my Dad was conflicted when St. Peter apprised him of the fact that she'd be sharing his space – happy to have her near-by, not so happy with her superior position, but for once, he couldn't say a damn thing.

He had been gone for over a decade when her health started to decline. One day she announced that she was moving out of state to live with my sister. You've been my angel for the last decade, she said, now it's your sister's turn. A year later she passed away.

My sister saw to the viewing and the actual cremation – thank God for that. Had that piece been entrusted to my distracted self she might still be waiting for her little gold-domed repository.

Anyway, my brother picked her up from my sister's, and delivered her to me for her final journey to Section H, Block 12, Lot 115.

It was at this point in my reverie that it occurred to me that my mother would have been incensed had I wasted my time with Rosie on her cemetery jaunt because she's not there. I don't mean in the existential sense – my mother really is not there.

She is still in my curio cabinet.

I'm sure she is ambivalent about her predicament. On the one hand, she is in a lovely living room decorated in a style very similar to her own with lots of company and laughter in the house. On the other hand, I, her hard-headed daughter, did not follow her instructions.

But on second thought I realized that if my mom were here to record a new tape she'd say, "Don't worry about the cemetery thing. You brought me flowers when I could smell them. Get on with your writing. I told you where I'd be."

ACKNOWLEDGMENTS

*I am indebted to those who said
you can't do it and those who said you can.
My deepest gratitude is to those
who insisted I get it done.*

Mary Lou Scalise Edwards was born into an Italian-American
culture with all its richness and idiosyncrasies. She grew up in
Bridgeport, a Chicago neighborhood steeped in the traditions
of politics and prejudice, home to mayors, mobsters and moguls.
At the University of Illinois she discovered that the whole world
was not Catholic.

Early on, her mother urged her to stay on the Honor Roll recognizing
that she had an aversion to four letter words like
I-R-O-N, C-O-O-K and D-U-S-T.

She resides in the metro-Chicago area with her husband and
a menagerie of critters.